Rail Guide

2019

Light Rail and Heritage Railways

Colin J. Marsden

Crécy Publishing Ltd

First published 2019 by Crécy Publishing

ISBN 978 1 9108 09563

Printed in Bulgaria by Multiprint

Crécy Publishing Ltd
1a Ringway Trading Estate
Shadowmoss Road
Manchester
M22 5LH
Tel +44 (0) 161 499 0024

www.crecy.co.uk

Front cover top: *A1X 0-6-0T No. W11* Newport *is seen working on the Isle of Wight Steam Railway at Havenstreet. In BR days, this loco was numbered 32640.* **CJM**

Front cover bottom: *In summer 2018 a start was made to applying the new West Midlands blue livery to the tram fleet. No. 31 at West Bromwich Central, displays the new colours.* **John Binch**

Back cover top: *Manx Electric Railway No. 9 this motor car was built in 1894 by G F Milnes of Birkenhead and is still in traffic today as one of the main vehicles working the Douglas to Ramsey service. On 30 July 2018 it is seen passing Ballaragh with trailer 47 heading towards Laxey.* **CJM**

Back cover bottom: *A London Underground Northern Line train, led by Driving Motor No. 51626 is recorded at Euston station.* **Antony Christie**

Acknowledgement – The Author would like to record his thanks to the many railway staff who have provided invaluable information for the production of this book. Also to the many photographers, especially Antony Christie, Nathan Williamson and John Binch, for providing many of the images. I would also like to express my thanks to Keith Ewins and Antony Christie for reading the updated manuscript. **CJM**

Welcome to the first edition of *ABC Rail Guide Light Rail and Heritage Railways*. Over the past decade we have included all information in one title, but with so many new train orders and fleet developments, compounded by the wish of readers to have expanded coverage of light rail systems, especially full numeric listings of London Underground stock, we have now split the Light Rail and Preservation sections from Rail Guide producing a stand alone title.

The interest in preserved railways and traction is huge and growing. For the first time, *ABC Rail Guide* is providing full details of preserved sites and railway museums, giving addresses and post codes for those visiting, together with a complete numeric listing of all preserved steam, diesel and electric locomotives, plus multiple unit stock.

In future editions of *ABC Rail Guide*, we plan to further extend coverage.

The largest Light Rail system in the UK is the London Underground network, covering both surface and tube lines, the system of 250 miles (402km) with 270 stations, using hundreds of multiple unit trains, is now covered on a line by line basis, providing basic route information and full stock details.

Over the last three decades, Light Rail has considerably expanded in the UK, following the opening of the first (non London) system in Tyne and Wear in 1980. Today, we have extensive and expanding systems operating in Edinburgh, Nottingham, Blackpool, Sheffield, Birmingham, Croydon and of course Docklands in London. The system in Edinburgh is about to be further extended south from the city, while work is ongoing to extend the Birmingham (Midland Metro), this will include battery powered street running in Birmingham City Centre to remove the need for unsightly overhead power lines.

In 2018, in Sheffield, the South Yorkshire SuperTram system was extended by the introduction of TramTrains on a new route between Sheffield Cathedral and Rotherham Parkgate, diverging from the original tram system at Tinsley / Meadowhall and joining the Network Rail infrastructure operated by Northern Rail via Rotherham Central to Rotherham Parkgate. This is currently being operated as a Government trial of TramTrain technology.

For completeness, *ABC Rail Guide Light Rail and Heritage Railways*, also covers some of the smaller, but nevertheless important systems, such as the Great Orme Tramway, Hythe Pier Tramway, Volks Electric Railway and the non-railway London cable-car operating in Docklands.

The world famous, Seaton Tramway in Devon is also included, while this is primarily a tourist attraction and uses tram replicas, it is an important tram system and provides good understanding of tram operations to younger visitors.

In the future, we plan to extend the coverage of *ABC Railguide* even further and would welcome any comments and suggestions from readers, please address these for the attention of the editor at the editorial address.

Enjoy your visits to the UK Light Railway systems and Preserved Railways, as always please keep your eyes about you, never trespass into areas which are not open to the public and if you see anything that causes you concern please report it. Enthusiasts and followers of the railways can provide an extra pair of eyes, so always be aware of what is going on around you.

Colin J. Marsden
Editor
February 2019

Rail Guide information is correct to 1 February 2019

Below: *Stadler/Vossloh 'TramTrain No. 201 (399201) passes through the high-level platforms at Rotherham Central with a 'TramTrain' service from Sheffield Cathedral to Rotherham Parkgate.* **CJM**

Contents

Transport For London (TFL) London Underground – P6 – 27

Lines: 6, New Stock: 7, Bakerloo Line: 8, Central Line: 10, Waterloo & City Line: 12, Piccadilly Line: 14, Northern Line: 16, Jubilee Line: 18, Victoria Line: 20, Circle, District and Hammersmith & City Lines: 21, Metropolitan Line: 24, Service Stock: 26.

Transport For London (TFL) Trams – P28 – 33

Croydon Tramlink: 28, Docklands Light Railway: 30, Emirates Air Line: 33.

Tramways – P34 – 57

Blackpool: 34, Edinburgh: 36, Glasgow Subway: 38, Manchester Metrolink: 40, West Midlands Metro: 42, Nottingham Express Transit: 44, South Yorkshire Supertram: 46, Tramtrain: 48, Tyne & Wear Metro: 50, Dublin LUAS: 52, Great Orme Tramway: 54, Hythe Pier Tramway: 54, Southend Pier Tramway: 55, Volks Electric Railway: 55, Seaton Tramway: 56.

Isle of Man Railways – P58 – 71

Manx Electric Railway: 58, Snaefell Mountain Railway: 63, Douglas Bay Horse Tramway: 64, Isle of Man Steam Railway: 66.

UK Heritage Railways – P72 – 110

Heritage Sites: 72, Railway Centres and Museums: 74, Preserved Modern Traction Locos: 80, Preserved Modern Traction DMUs: 85, Preserved Modern Traction SRDEMUs: 87, Preserved Modern Traction EMUs: 88, Preserved Steam Locomotives: 98, Main Line Certified Locomotives: 105.

Data – P111

Preserved Site Codes: 111.

Right: *Isle of Man Railways 1908-built Beyer Peacock 2-4-0T No. 12* Hutchinson *powers a five-coach Douglas to Port Erin service at Blackboards Bridge on 1 August 2018.* **CJM**

Below: *Former Great Western Railway 3200 Class 'Dukedog' No. 9017* Earl of Berkeley *is resident on the Bluebell Railway, and is seen painted in BR black livery at Horsted Keynes in spring 2018.* **Antony Christie**

Transport for London London Underground

Address: ✉ Floor 11, Windsor House, 50 Victoria Street, London, SW1H 0TL
pressoffice@tfl.gov.uk
✆ 0845 604 4141
ⓘ www.tfl.gov.uk

Managing Director: Mark Wild; Gareth Powell - Sub-surface lines

Operations: The London Underground system, now operated by Transport for London (TfL), operates services on 10 lines in and around the capital and uses a mix of surface and tunnel stock.

Bakerloo Line	Tube Line. Operates between Elephant & Castle and Harrow & Wealdstone. **Rolling Stock:** 1972 Mk2, livery - red, white and blue, allocated to Stonebridge Park. Scheduled for replacement in 2018-19.
Central Line	Tube Line. Operates services between West Ruislip/Ealing and Epping. **Rolling Stock:** 1992, livery - red, white and blue, allocated to Hainault.
Circle Line	Sub-Surface Line. Operates circle network in Central London and the branch from Edgware Road to Hammersmith. **Rolling Stock:** 'S' stock, introduced 2013-14, livery - red, white and blue, allocated to Hammersmith.
District Line	Sub-Surface Line. Operates services between Wimbledon, Richmond, Ealing, Edgware Road, Kensington Olympia and Upminster. **Rolling Stock:** 'S' stock, livery - red, white and blue, allocated to Ealing Common and Upminster.
Jubilee Line	Tube Line. Operates services between Stanmore and Stratford. **Rolling Stock:** 1996, livery - red, white and blue, allocated to Wembley Park.
Metropolitan Line	Sub-Surface Line. Operates services from Amersham, Chesham, Watford and Uxbridge to Aldgate. **Rolling Stock:** 'S', livery - red, white and blue, allocated to Wembley Park.
Northern Line	Tube Line. Operates services between Morden and Edgware, Mill Hill East and High Barnet. **Rolling Stock:** 1995 stock, livery - red, white and blue, allocated to Morden.
Piccadilly Line	Tube Line. Operates between Heathrow Airport/Uxbridge and Cockfosters. **Rolling Stock:** 1973 stock, livery - red, white and blue, allocated to Northfields and Cockfosters.
Victoria Line	Tube Line. Operates services between Brixton and Walthamstow Central. **Rolling Stock:** 2009 stock, livery - red, white and blue, allocated to Northumberland Park.
Waterloo & City Line	Tube Line. Operates services between Waterloo and Bank. **Rolling Stock:** 1992 stock, livery - red, white and blue, allocated to Waterloo.
Hammersmith & City	Sub-Surface Line. Operates between Hammersmith and Barking. **Rolling Stock:** 'S', livery - red, white and blue

New Tube Stock for London Underground

It was announced on 15 June 2018, that Siemens Mobility had been awarded the contract, valued at around £1.5bn to design and build 94 new generation tube trains, based on the 'Inspiro' platform, that will transform the experience of millions of London Underground passengers, with those on the Piccadilly line the first to benefit.

More than 700,000 passengers use the Piccadilly line every day. However, a combination of limited fleet size and old infrastructure has restricted TfL's ability to increase capacity across the line for many decades. This long-term investment will support London's growing population which is set to increase to 10.8 million by 2041.

Twenty two UK suppliers have been identified in the bid to potentially work with Siemens Mobility on the build project. The trains will be built at a new Siemens factory in Goole, East Yorkshire, where dynamic commission facilities will also be built. The trains will then be delivered to London Underground by rail. The new Siemens plant will employ around 700 people.

The Siemens order, the first under the LUL Deep Tube Upgrade Programme – will mean the replacement of the entire 1970s built Piccadilly line fleet. From 2023, 94 new trains will be delivered, enabling up to 27 trains-per-hour to operate at peak times by the end of 2026.

The four deep tube lines make up a third of the Underground network, carrying around two million passengers per day on key corridors linking the City, the West End, King's Cross and Heathrow Airport.

The Deep Tube Upgrade Programme aims to replace the life-expired rolling stock, signalling and control systems across all the four lines, with completion by 2035.

The Siemens 'Inspiro' trains will be six metres longer than existing Piccadilly stock, they will include walk-through, fully air conditioned carriages, and will be designed to optimise the space constraints in the narrow tube tunnels. The stock will also be fitted with in-train information systems.

Although the initial order for 94 trains is for the Piccadilly Line, it is expected a single manufacturer will build the trains for all four tube lines. This will allow TfL to maximise cost savings through greater standardisation, including staff training, equipment, spares and maintenance. ■

Above: *Artists impression on how the new deep tube stock will look. The first line to see the new 'standard' deep tube trains will be the Piccadilly Line.* **LUL**

BAKERLOO LINE

1972 Tube Stock

Builder: Metro-Cammell
Years built: 1972-1974
Formation: DM+T+T+MM+UNDM+T+DM
Construction: Steel underframe, aluminium body
Max speed: 45mph (72km/h)
Length: Cab - 52ft 8in (16.09m),
Intermediate - 52ft 4in (15.98m)
Width: 8ft 6in (2.64m)

Height: 9ft 4in (2.87m)
Gangway:Emergency end doors
Seating: Total 268
DM-40, T-36, MM-40, UNDM-40
Doors: Sliding bi-parting
Traction equipment: 4 x Brush LT115 of 71hp (53kW) on each power car

4-car single-ended sets (formed at south end of train)

Formation: (South end) DM+T+T+MM

**3231+4231+4331+3331
3232+4232+4332+3332
3233+4233+4333+3333
3234+4234+4334+3334
3235+4235+4335+3335
3236+4236+4336+3336
3237+4237+4337+3337
3238+4238+4338+3338
3239+4239+4339+3339
3240+4240+4340+3340
3241+4241+4341+3341
3242+4242+4342+3342
3243+4243+4343+3343
3244+4244+4344+3344
3245+4245+4345+3345
3246+4246+4346+3346
3247+4247+4347+3347
3248+4248+4348+3348
3250+4250+4350+3350
3251+4251+4351+3351
3252+4252+4352+3352
3253+4253+4353+3353
3254+4254+4354+3354
3255+4255+4355+3355
3256+4256+4356+3356
3258+4258+4358+3358
3259+4259+4359+3359
3260+4260+4360+3360
3261+4261+4361+3361
3262+4262+4362+3362
3263+4263+4363+3363
3264+4264+4364+3364
3265+4265+4365+3365
3266+4266+4366+3366
3267+4267+4367+3367
3299+4299+4399+3399***

3-car single-ended sets (formed at north end of train)

Formation: UNDM+T+DM (North end)

**3431+4531+3531
3432+4532+3532
3433+4533+3533
3434+4534+3534
3435+4535+3535
3436+4536+3536
3437+4537+3537
3438+4538+3538
3440+4540+3540
3441+4541+3541
3442+4542+3542
3443+4543+3543
3444+4544+3544
3445+4545+3545
3446+4546+3546
3447+4547+3547
3448+4548+3548
3449+4549+3549
3450+4550+3550
3451+4551+3551
3452+4552+3552
3453+4553+3553
3454+4554+3554
3455+4555+3555
3456+4556+3556
3457+4557+3557
3458+4558+3558
3459+4559+3559
3460+4560+3560
3461+4561+3561
3462+4562+3562
3463+4563+3563
3464+4564+3564
3465+4565+3565
3466+4566+3566
3467+4567+3567**

Notes: Nos. 4352-4363 fittted with de-icing equipment.
* UNDM vehicle

Left: *Built between 1972-1974, the 1972-Stock deployed on the Bakerloo Line is operated by a fleet of 36 seven-car sets, each train formed of a four and three-car set. Driving Motor No. 3263 leads a train at Stonebridge Park.* **Antony Christie**

Above: *The Bakerloo Line is operated with the three-car sets formed at the north end of the train and the four car set at the south. North facing DM No. 3545 is illustrated at Stonebridge Park.* **Antony Christie**

Right Middle: *Bakerloo Line services north of Queens Park as far as Harrow & Wealdstone operate over the Network Rail Euston-Watford DC lines which are equipped for fourth rail operation. A southbound Bakerloo train is seen approaching Willesden Junction low level, led by DM No. 3247.* **CJM**

Right Below: *Bakerloo Line 1972 stock interior, showing 2019 refurbished condition.* **CJM**

CENTRAL LINE

1992 Tube Stock

Builder: ADtranz
Years built: 1991-1994
Formation: DM+M+M+M+M+M+M+DM
Construction: Aluminium
Max speed: 53mph (85km/h)
Length: 53ft 3in (16.25m)
Width: 8ft 5½in (2.62m)

Height: 9ft 4in (2.87m)
Gangway: Emergency end doors
Seating: Total 272
DM-34, NDM-34
Doors: Sliding bi-parting
Traction equipment: 4 x Brush LT118 of 65hp (49kW) on each power car

2-car single-ended sets

Formation: A+B - DM+NDM

91001+92001
91003+92003
91005+92005
91007+92007
91009+92009
91011+92011
91013+92013
91015+92015
91017+92017
91019+92019
91021+92021
91023+92023
91025+92025
91027+92027
91029+92029
91031+92031
91033+92033
91035+92035
91037+92037
91039+92039
91041+92041
91043+92043
91045+92045
91047+92047
91049+92049
91051+92051
91053+92053
91055+92055
91057+92057
91059+92059
91061+92061
91063+92063
91065+92065
91067+92067
91069+92069
91071+92071
91073+92073
91075+92075
91077+92077
91079+92079
91081+92081
91083+92083
91085+92085
91087+92087
91089+92089
91091+92091
91093+92093
91095+92095
91097+92097
91099+92099
91101+92101
91103+92103
91105+92105
91107+92107
91109+92109
91111+92111
91113+92113
91115+92115
91117+92117
91119+92119
91121+92121
91123+92123
91125+92125
91127+92127
91129+92129
91131+92131
91133+92133
91135+92135
91137+92137
91139+92139
91141+92141
91143+92143
91145+92145
91147+92147
91149+92149
91151+92151
91153+92153
91155+92155
91157+92157
91159+92159
91161+92161
91163+92163
91165+92165
91167+92167
91169+92169
91171+92171
91173+92173
91175+92175
91177+92177
91179+92179
91181+92181
91183+92183
91185+92185
91187+92187
91189+92189
91191+92191
91193+92193
91195+92195
91197+92197
91199+92199
91201+92201
91203+92203
91205+92205
91207+92207
91209+92209
91211+92211
91213+92213
91215+92215
91217+92217
91219+92219
91221+92221
91223+92223
91225+92225
91227+92227
91229+92229
91231+92231
91233+92233
91235+92235
91237+92237
91239+92239
91241+92241
91243+92243
91245+92245
91247+92247
91249+92249
91251+92251
91253+92253
91255+92255
91257+92257
91259+92259
91261+92261
91263+92263
91265+92265
91267+92267
91269+92269
91271+92271
91273+92273
91275+92275
91277+92277
91279+92279
91281+92281
91283+92283
91285+92285
91287+92287
91289+92289
91291+92291
91293+92293
91295+92295
91297+92297
91299+92299
91301+92301
91303+92303
91305+92305
91307+92307
91309+92309
91311+92311
91313+92313
91315+92315
91317+92317
91319+92319
91321+92321
91323+92323
91325+92325
91327+92327
91329+92329
91331+92331
91333+92333
91335+92335
91337+92337
91339+92339
91341+92341
91343+92343
91345+92345
91347+92347
91349+92349

2-car non-driving sets

Formation: B+C - NDM+NDM

92002+93002
92004+93004
92006+93006
92008+93008
92010+93010
92012+93012
92014+93014
92016+93016
92018+93018
92020+93020
92022+93022
92024+93024
92026+93026
92028+93028
92030+93030
92032+93032
92034+93034
92036+93036
92038+93038
92040+93040
92042+93042
92044+93044
92046+93046
92048+93048
92050+93050
92052+93052
92054+93054
92056+93056
92058+93058
92060+93060
92062+93062
92064+93064
92066+93066
92068+93068
92070+93070
92072+93072
92074+93074
92076+93076
92078+93078
92080+93080
92082+93082
92084+93084
92086+93086
92088+93088
92090+93090
92092+93092
92094+93094
92096+93096
92098+93098
92100+93100
92102+93102
92104+93104
92106+93106
92108+93108
92110+93110
92112+93112
92114+93114
92116+93116
92118+93118
92120+93120

92122+93122
92124+93124
92126+93126
92128+93128
92130+93130
92132+93132
92134+93134
92136+93136
92138+93138
92140+93140
92142+93142
92144+93144
92146+93146
92148+93148
92150+93150
92152+93152
92154+93154
92156+93156
92158+93158
92160+93160
92162+93162
92164+93164
92166+93166
92168+93168
92170+93170
92172+93172
92174+93174
92176+93176
92178+93178
92180+93180
92182+93182
92184+93184
92186+93186
92188+93188
92190+93190
92192+93192
92194+93194
92196+93196
92198+93198
92200+93200
92202+93202
92204+93204
92206+93206
92208+93208
92210+93210
92212+93212
92214+93214
92216+93216
92218+93218
92220+93220
92222+93222
92224+93224
92226+93226
92228+93228
92230+93230
92232+93232
92234+93234
92236+93236
92238+93238
92240+93240
92242+93242
92244+93244
92246+93246
92248+93248
92250+93250
92252+93252
92254+93254
92256+93256
92258+93258
92260+93260
92262+93262
92264+93264
92266+93266

2-car non-driving sets

Formation: B+D - NDM+NDM

92402+93402
92404+93404
92406+93406
92408+93408
92410+93410
92412+93412
92414+93414
92416+93416
92418+93418
92420+93420
92422+93422
92424+93424
92426+93426
92428+93428
92430+93430
92432+93432
92434+93434
92436+93436
92438+93438
92440+93440
92442+93442
92444+93444
92446+93446
92448+93448
92450+93450
92452+93452
92454+93454
92456+93456
92458+93458
92460+93460
92462+93462
92464+93464

Right: *The 46 mile (79km) Central Line with 49 stations is operated by a fleet of AdTranz-built 1992 tube stock, with trains formed of eight-cars (4x2). Driving Motor No. 91243 is seen leading a train at Epping.* **Antony Christie**

Below: *Type 'A' car Driving Motor No. 91037 is seen leading a formation into Greenford station. The Central Line operates east-west through central London from West Ruislip/Ealing Broadway in the west to Hainault/ Epping in the east.* **Antony Christie**

WATERLOO & CITY LINE

1992 Tube Stock

Builder: ADtranz
Years built: 1993
Formation: DM+M+M+DM
Construction: Aluminium
Max speed: 53mph (85km/h)
Length: 53ft 3in (16.25m)
Width: 8ft 5½in (2.62m)

Height: 9ft 4in (2.87m)
Gangway: Emergency end doors
Seating: Total 136
DM-34, M-34
Doors: Sliding bi-parting
Traction equipment: 4 x Brush LT118 of 65hp (49kW) on each power car

2-car sets - east

Formation: DM+M

65501+67501
65503+67503
65505+67505
65507+67507
65509+67509

2-car sets - west

Formation: M+DM

67502+65502
67504+65504
67506+65506
67508+65508
67510+65510

Left Above: *The shortest of the London Underground lines is the Waterloo & City Line, linking Waterloo and Bank stations at just 1.47miles (2.37km) The line has no intermediate stations and until 1 April 1994 was operated by BR Southern Railway/ Region. In April 1994 it was sold to London Underground. With its depot at Waterloo the line is operated by a fleet of ten 2-car trains formed into five four-car sets. DM No. 65504 is seen nearest the camera at Waterloo after arriving from Bank.*
Antony Christie

Left Below: *Interior of Waterloo and City stock. These sets were constructed by AdTranz, Derby Litchurch Lane Works as an add-on order to the Central Line fleet. Internal trim uses the lines turquoise colour. A four-car train has seating for 136, but in the peak period trains can carry five times that number of passengers. Each year some 16 million passengers use the route.* **Antony Christie**

Above: *Two platforms exist at Bank station, both serving for arriving and departing services, in peak periods, platforms are used alternatively to speed loading and departures. A train led by DM 65505 is seen arriving at Bank.* **CJM**

Right: *During peak periods, the Waterloo & City lines operates every four minutes, and even with this frequency, passengers are frequently left waiting for the next train. DM No. 65501 forms the rear vehicle of a departing train from Bank bound for Waterloo.* **Antony Christie**

Left: *The Waterloo & City Line being a self contained operation with no connection to any other line, has its own maintenance facility at Waterloo, where all stock can be stabled. If trains are required to be removed from the line, a lifting hole is provided adjacent to the depot where stock can be craned out and removed by road. DM No. 65503 is illustrated arriving in the Bank bound platform at Waterloo from the depot.* **Antony Christie**

PICCADILLY LINE

1973 Tube Stock

Builder: Metro Cammell
Years built: 1974-1977
Formation: DM+T+UNDM+UNDM+T+DM or
DM+T+UNDM+DM+T+DM
Construction: Steel underframe, aluminium body
Max speed: 45mph (72km/h)
Length: Cab - 57ft 3in (17.47m)
Intermediate - 58ft 0in (17.68m)

Width: 8ft 5¾in (2.63m)
Height: 9ft 4in (2.88m)
Gangway: Emergency end doors
Seating: Total 228
DM-38, T-38, UNDM-38
Doors: Sliding bi-parting
Traction equipment: 4 x Brush LT118 of 65hp (49kW) on each power car

3-car single-ended sets

Formation: DM+T+UNDM

100+500+300
101+501+301
102+502+302
103+503+303
104+504+304
105+505+305
106+506+306
107+507+307
108+508+308
109+509+309
110+510+310
111+511+311
112+512+312
113+513+313
115+515+315
116+516+316
117+517+317
118+518+318
119+519+319
120+520+320
121+521+321
122+522+322
123+523+323
124+524+324
125+525+325
126+526+326
127+527+327
128+528+328
129+529+329
130+530+330
131+531+331
132+532+332
133+533+333
134+534+334
135+535+335
136+536+336
137+537+337
138+538+338
139+539+339
140+540+340
141+541+341
142+542+342
143+543+343
144+544+344
145+545+345
146+546+346
147+547+347
148+548+348
149+549+349
150+550+350
151+551+351
152+552+352
153+553+353
154+554+354
155+555+355
156+556+356
157+557+357
158+558+358
159+559+359
160+560+360
161+561+361
162+562+362
163+563+363
164+564+364
165+565+365
166+566+366 (Bomb dam)
167+567+367
168+568+368
169+569+369
170+570+370
171+571+371
172+572+372
173+573+373
174+574+374
175+575+375
176+576+376
177+577+377
178+578+378
179+579+379
180+580+380
181+581+381
182+582+382
183+583+383
184+584+384
185+585+385
186+586+386
187+587+387
188+588+388
189+589+389
190+590+390
191+591+391
192+592+392
193+593+393
194+594+394
195+595+395
196+596+396
197+597+397
198+598+398
199+599+399
200+600+400
201+601+401
202+602+402
203+603+403
205+605+405
206+606+406
207+607+407
208+608+408
209+609+409
210+610+410
211+611+411
212+612+412
213+613+413
214+614+414
215+615+415
216+616+416
217+617+417
218+618+418
219+619+419
220+620+420
221+621+421
222+622+422
223+623+423
224+624+424
225+625+425
226+626+426
227+627+427
228+628+428
229+629+429
230+630+430
231+631+431
232+632+432
233+633+433
234+634+434
235+635+435
236+636+436
237+637+437
238+638+438
239+639+439
240+640+440
241+641+441
242+642+442
243+643+443
244+644+444
245+645+445
246+646+446
247+647+447
248+648+448
249+649+449
250+650+450
251+651+451
252+652+452
253+653+453

3-car double-ended sets

Formation: DM+T+DM

854+654+855
856+656+857
858+658+859
860+660+861
862+662+863
864+664+865
866+666+867
868+668+869
870+670+871
872+672+873
874+674+875
876+676+877
878+678+879
880+680+881
882+682+883
884+684+885
886+686+887
890+690+891
892+692+893
894+694+895
896+696+897

Right: *The 44mile (71km) Piccadilly line with 53 stations is another west-east running line, operating from Uxbridge/Heathrow in the west to Cockfosters in the east. With 210million passengers this is the fourth busiest London Underground line. The line is operated by a fleet of 86 six-car 1973 trains, of which 79 are required to maintain the peak service. Led by DM No. 189 an Uxbridge bound train is seen at Alperton.* **Antony Christie**

Left: *On the left is car No. 860 a Driving Motor from a three-car double ended set, while on the right is car No. 106 a Driving Motor from a single ended three-car unit. The trains meet at Rayners Lane station.*
Antony Christie

Below: *Double ended driving Motor car No. 860, coupled to a UNDM vehicle of a single ended three-car unit. Note the fabric curtain coupled between cars to reduce the risk of passengers trying to go between vehicles.*
Antony Christie

Light Rail

NORTHERN LINE

1995 Tube Stock

Builder: GEC Alstom
Years built: 1996-2000
Formation: DM+T+UNDM+UNDM+T+DM
Construction: Aluminium
Max speed: 45mph (72km/h)
Length: 58ft 2in (17.77m)
Width: 8ft 5¾in (2.63m)
Height: 9ft 4in (2.87m)
Gangway: Emergency end doors
Seating: Total 200
DM-32, T-38, T-34, UNDM-34
Doors: Sliding bi-parting
Traction equipment: 4 x GEC G355AZ of 114hp (85kW) on each power car

6-car double-ended sets

Formation: DM+T+UNDM+UNDM+T+DM

51501+52501+53501+53701+52701+51701
51502+52502+53502+53503+52503+51503
51504+52504+53504+53505+52505+51505
51506+52506+53506+53507+52507+51507
51508+52508+53508+53702+52702+51702
51509+52509+53509+53510+52510+51510
51511+52511+53511+53512+52512+51512
51513+52513+53513+53514+52514+51514
51515+52515+53515+53703+52703+51703
51516+52516+53516+53517+52517+51517
51518+52518+53518+53519+52519+51519
51520+52520+53520+53704+52704+51704
51521+52521+53521+53522+52522+51522
51523+52523+53523+53524+52524+51524
51525+52525+53525+53705+52705+51705
51526+52526+53526+53527+52527+51527
51528+52528+53528+53529+52529+51529
51530+52530+53530+53531+52531+51531
51532+52532+53532+53706+52706+51706
51533+52533+53533+53534+52534+51534
51535+52535+53535+53536+52536+51536
51537+52537+53537+53538+52538+51538
51539+52539+53539+53707+52707+51707
51540+52540+53540+53541+52541+51541
51542+52542+53542+53543+52543+51543
51544+52544+53544+53545+52545+51545
51546+52546+53546+53708+52708+51708
51547+52547+53547+53548+52548+51548
51549+52549+53549+53550+52550+51550
51551+52551+53551+53711+52711+51711
51553+52553+53553+53709+52709+51709
51554+52554+53554+53555+52555+51555
51556+52556+53556+53557+52557+51557
51558+52558+53558+53559+52559+51559
51560+52560+53560+53710+52710+51710
51561+52561+53561+53562+52562+51562
51563+52563+53563+53564+52564+51564
51565+52565+53565+53566+52566+51566
51567+52567+53567+53552+52552+51552
51568+52568+53568+53569+52569+51569
51570+52570+53570+53571+52571+51571
51572+52572+53572+53573+52573+51573
51574+52574+53574+53712+52712+51712
51575+52575+53575+53576+52576+51576
51577+52577+53577+53578+52578+51578
51579+52579+53579+53580+52580+51580
51581+52581+53581+53713+52713+51713
51582+52582+53582+53583+52583+51583
51584+52584+53584+53585+52585+51585
51586+52586+53586+53587+52587+51587
51588+52588+53588+53714+52714+51714
51589+52589+53589+53590+52590+51590
51591+52591+53591+53592+52592+51592
51593+52593+53593+53594+52594+51594
51595+52595+53595+53715+52715+51715
51596+52596+53596+53597+52597+51597
51598+52598+53598+53599+52599+51599
51600+52600+53600+53601+52601+51601
51602+52602+53602+53716+52716+51716
51603+52603+53603+53604+52604+51604
51605+52605+53605+53606+52606+51606
51607+52607+53607+53608+52608+51608
51609+52609+53609+53717+52717+51717
51610+52610+53610+53611+52611+51611
51612+52612+53612+53613+52613+51613
51614+52614+53614+53615+52615+51615
51616+52616+53616+53718+52718+51718
51617+52617+53617+53618+52618+51618
51619+52619+53619+53620+52620+51620
51621+52621+53621+53622+52622+51622
51623+52623+53623+53719+52719+51719
51624+52624+53624+53625+52625+51625
51626+52626+53626+53627+52627+51627
51628+52628+53628+53629+52629+51629
51630+52630+53630+53720+52720+51720
51631+52631+53631+53632+52632+51632
51633+52633+53633+53634+52634+51634
51635+52635+53635+53636+52636+51636
51637+52637+53637+53721+52721+51721
51638+52638+53638+53639+52639+51639
51640+52640+53640+53641+52641+51641
51642+52642+53642+53643+52643+51643
51644+52644+53644+53722+52722+51722
51645+52645+53645+53646+52646+51646
51647+52647+53647+53648+52648+51648
51649+52649+53649+53650+52650+51650
51651+52651+53651+53723+52723+51723
51652+52652+53652+53653+52653+51653
51654+52654+53654+53655+52655+51655
51656+52656+53656+53657+52657+51657
51658+52658+53658+53724+52724+51724
51659+52659+53659+53660+52660+51660
51661+52661+53661+53662+52662+51662
51663+52663+53663+53664+52664+51664
51665+52665+53665+53725+52725+51725
51666+52666+53666+53667+52667+51667
51668+52668+53668+53669+52669+51669
51670+52670+53670+53671+52671+51671
51672+52672+53672+53726+52726+51726
51673+52673+53673+53674+52674+51674

51675+52675+53675+53676+52676+51676
51677+52677+53677+53678+52678+51678
51679+52679+53679+53680+52680+51680
51681+52681+53681+53682+52682+51682
51683+52683+53683+53684+52684+51684
51685+52685+53685+53686+52686+51686

Above: *A fleet of 106 six-car GEC-Alstom built sets operate the 36mile (58km) Northern Line, running north-south through London from Edgware/ Mill Hill East/High Barnet in the north to Morden in the south. Led by Driving Motor No. 51560 a train is seen at West Finchley.* **Antony Christie**

Right: *Led by driving Motor No. 51626 a Northern Line service is seen in the tunnel section at Euston.* **Antony Christie**

Below: *Line up of Northern Line trains at Finchley Central with left to right Nos. 51628, 51640 and 51616.* **Antony Christie**

JUBILEE LINE

1996 Tube Stock

Builder: GEC Alstom, CAF Spain§
Years built: 1996-1998, 2005§
Formation: DM+T+T+UNDM+UNDM+T+DM
Construction: Aluminium
Max speed: 62mph (100km/h)
Length: 58ft 2in (17.77m)
Width: 8ft 5¾in (2.63m)
Height: 9ft 4in (2.87m)
Gangway: Emergency end doors
Seating: Total 238
DM-32, T-34, UNDM-34
Doors: Sliding bi-parting
Traction equipment: 4 x GEC LT200 of 120hp (90kW) on each power car

4-car Single-ended sets. Formation: DM+T+T§+UNDM

96001+96201+96601+96401
96003+96203+96603+96403
96005+96205+96605+96405
96007+96207+96607+96407
96009+96209+96609+96409
96011+96211+96611+96411
96013+96213+96613+96413
96015+96215+96615+96415
96017+96217+96617+96417
96019+96219+96619+96419
96021+96221+96621+96421
96023+96223+96623+96423
96025+96225+96625+96425
96027+96227+96627+96427
96029+96229+96629+96429
96031+96231+96631+96431
96033+96233+96633+96433
96035+96235+96635+96435
96037+96237+96637+96437
96039+96239+96639+96439
96041+96241+96641+96441
96043+96243+96643+96443
96045+96245+96645+96445
96047+96247+96647+96447
96049+96249+96649+96449
96051+96251+96651+96451
96053+96253+96653+96453
96055+96255+96655+96455
96057+96257+96657+96457
96059+96259+96659+96459
96061+96261+96661+96461
96063+96263+96663+96463
96065+96265+96665+96465
96067+96267+96667+96467
96069+96269+96669+96469
96071+96271+96671+96471
96073+96273+96673+96473
96075+96275+96675+96475
96077+96277+96677+96477
96079+96279+96679+96479
96081+96281+96681+96481
96083+96283+96683+96483
96085+96285+96685+96485
96087+96287+96687+96487
96089+96289+96689+96489
96091+96291+96691+96491
96093+96293+96693+96493
96095+96295+96695+96495
96097+96297+96697+96497
96099+96299+96699+96499
96101+96301+96701+96501
96103+96303+96703+96503
96105+96305+96705+96505
96107+96307+96707+96507
96109+96309+96709+96509
96111+96311+96711+96511
96113+96313+96713+96513
96115+96315+96715+96515
96117+96317+96717+96517
§96119+96319+96719+96519
§96121+96321+96721+96521
§96123+96323+96723+96523
§96125+96325+96725+96525

3-car Single-ended sets. Formation: DM+T+UNDM

96402+96202+96002
96404+96204+96004
96406+96206+96006
96408+96208+96008
96410+96210+96010
96412+96212+96012
96414+96214+96014
96416+96216+96016
96418+96218+96018
96420+96220+96020
96422+96222+96022
96424+96224+96024
96426+96226+96026
96428+96228+96028
96430+96230+96030
96432+96232+96032
96434+96234+96034
96436+96236+96036
96438+96238+96038
96440+96240+96040
96442+96242+96042
96444+96244+96044
96446+96246+96046
96448+96248+96048
96450+96250+96050
96452+96252+96052
96454+96254+96054
96456+96256+96056
96458+96258+96058
96460+96260+96060
96462+96262+96062
96464+96264+96064
96466+96266+96066
96468+96268+96068
96470+96270+96070
96472+96272+96072
96474+96274+96074
96476+96276+96076
96478+96278+96078
96480+96280+96080
96482+96282+96082
96484+96284+96084
96486+96286+96086
96488+96288+96088
96490+96290+96090
96492+96292+96092
96494+96294+96094
96496+96296+96096
96498+96298+96098
96500+96300+96100
96502+96302+96102
96504+96304+96104
96506+96306+96106
96508+96308+96108
96510+96310+96110
96512+96312+96112
96514+96314+96114
96516+96316+96116
96518+96318+96118
§96520+96320+96120
§96522+96322+96122
§96524+96324+96124
§96526+96326+96126

Left: *Intermediate UNDM vehicle No. 96403 of Alstom-built four car 1996 Jubilee set, attached on the left to a like type vehicle from a three-car set. These vehicles seat 34 with room for around four times that number standing. Two single and two bi-parting sliding doors are provided on each side.*
Antony Christie

Above: *The 22.5mile (36.2km) Jubilee Line with 27 stations is operated by 63 seven-car 1996 Alstom-built trains, based at Stratford High Street depot. The line operates from Stanmore to Stratford via central London and in peak hours has 30 train paths per hour in the core North Greenwich-Willesden Green section. Led by DM No. 96003 a set is seen at Stratford Low Level station.* **Antony Christie**

Below: *Each seven-car Jubilee Line train has seating for 238 in the standard longitudinal style, however train accommodation in peak times is well over 1,200 people. Led by DM No. 96126 a formation is seen at Wembley Park.* **Antony Christie**

VICTORIA LINE

2009 Tube Stock

Builder: Bombardier, Derby
Years built: 2009-2011
Formation: DM+T+NDM+UNDM+UNDM+NDM+T+DM
Construction: Aluminium
Max speed: 50mph (80.5km/h)
Length: Driving - 54ft 4in (16.60m)
Intermediate - 53ft 6in (16.35m)
Width: 8ft 5½in (2.61m)

Height: 9ft 4⅜in (2.88m)
Gangway: Emergency end doors
Seating: Total 252
DM-32, T-32, NDM-32, UNDM-30
Doors: Sliding bi-parting
Traction equipment: 4 x Bombardier Mitrac of 100hp (75kW) on each power car

8-car Double-ended sets

Formation: DM (north)+T+NDM+UNDM+UNDM+NDM+T+DM (south)

11001+12001+13001+14001+14002+13002+12002+11002
11003+12003+13003+14003+14004+13004+12004+11004
11005+12005+13005+14005+14006+13006+12006+11006
11007+12007+13007+14007+14008+13008+12008+11008
11009+12009+13009+14009+14010+13010+12010+11010
11011+12011+13011+14011+14012+13012+12012+11012
11013+12013+13013+14013+14014+13014+12014+11014
11015+12015+13015+14015+14016+13016+12016+11016
11017+12017+13017+14017+14018+13018+12018+11018
11019+12019+13019+14019+14020+13020+12020+11020
11021+12021+13021+14021+14022+13022+12022+11022
11023+12023+13023+14023+14024+13024+12024+11024
11025+12025+13025+14025+14026+13026+12026+11026
11027+12027+13027+14027+14028+13028+12028+11028
11029+12029+13029+14029+14030+13030+12030+11030
11031+12031+13031+14031+14032+13032+12032+11032
11033+12033+13033+14033+14034+13034+12034+11034
11035+12035+13035+14035+14036+13036+12036+11036
11037+12037+13037+14037+14038+13038+12038+11038
11039+12039+13039+14039+14040+13040+12040+11040
11041+12041+13041+14041+14042+13042+12042+11042
11043+12043+13043+14043+14044+13044+12044+11044
11045+12045+13045+14045+14046+13046+12046+11046
11047+12047+13047+14047+14048+13048+12048+11048
11049+12049+13049+14049+14050+13050+12050+11050
11051+12051+13051+14051+14052+13052+12052+11052
11053+12053+13053+14053+14054+13054+12054+11054
11055+12055+13055+14055+14056+13056+12056+11056
11057+12057+13057+14057+14058+13058+12058+11058
11059+12059+13059+14059+14060+13060+12060+11060
11061+12061+13061+14061+14062+13062+12062+11062
11063+12063+13063+14063+14064+13064+12064+11064
11065+12065+13065+14065+14066+13066+12066+11066
11067+12067+13067+14067+14068+13068+12068+11068
11069+12069+13069+14069+14070+13070+12070+11070
11071+12071+13071+14071+14072+13072+12072+11072
11073+12073+13073+14073+14074+13074+12074+11074
11075+12075+13075+14075+14076+13076+12076+11076
11077+12077+13077+14077+14078+13078+12078+11078
11079+12079+13079+14079+14080+13080+12080+11080
11081+12081+13081+14081+14082+13082+12082+11082
11083+12083+13083+14083+14084+13084+12084+11084
11085+12085+13085+14085+14086+13086+12086+11086
11087+12087+13087+14087+14088+13088+12088+11088
11089+12089+13089+14089+14090+13090+12090+11090
11091+12091+13091+14091+14092+13092+12092+11092
11093+12093+13093+14093+14094+13094+12094+11094

Left: *A fleet of 47 eight-car Bombardier-built sets, classified as 2009 stock operate the Victoria Line. This line is 13 miles (21km) in length with 16 stations linking Walthamstow Central with Brixton via central London. The lines depot is at Northumberland Park. Led by driving Motor (North) No. 11079, a train is seen arriving at Vauxhall station.* **Antony Christie**

Right: *The Victoria line sees around 200 million journeys every year. The line, opened in the 1960s is currently operated under an Automatic Train Operation system supplied by Westinghouse replacing the original automated system. Currently 33 trains per hour can operate under the ATO system. Car No. 11015 trails a formation away from Seven Sisters.* **Antony Christie**

CIRCLE LINE | DISTRICT LINE | HAMMERSMITH & CITY LINE

S7 Sub-Surface Stock

Builder: Bombardier, Derby
Years built: 2011-2015
Formation: DM+M1+MS+MS+M2+M1+DM
Construction: Aluminium
Max speed: 62mph (100km/h)
Length: Driving - 57ft 2in (17.44m)
Intermediate - 50ft 6in (15.43m)
Width: 9ft 5in (2.92m)
Height: 12ft 0in (3.68m)
Gangway: Emergency end doors
Seating: Total 212
DM-32, M1-30, M2-30, MS-29
Doors: Sliding bi-parting
Traction equipment: 4 x Bombardier MJB20093 of 87hp (65kW) on each power car

7-car Double-ended sets

Formation: DM+M1+MS+MS+M2+M1+DM

21301+22301+24301+24302+25302+22302+21302
21303+22303+24303+24304+25304+22304+21304
21305+22305+24305+24306+25306+22306+21306
21307+22307+24307+24308+25308+22308+21308
21309+22309+24309+24310+25310+22310+21310
21311+22311+24311+24312+25312+22312+21312
21313+22313+24313+24314+25314+22314+21314
21315+22315+24315+24316+25316+22316+21316
21317+22317+24317+24318+25318+22318+21318
21319+22319+24319+24320+25320+22320+21320
21321+22321+24321+24322+25322+22322+21322
21325+22325+24325+24326+25326+22326+21326
21329+22329+24329+24330+25330+22330+21330
21331+22331+24331+24332+25332+22332+21332
21333+22333+24333+24334+25334+22334+21334
21335+22335+24335+24336+25336+22336+21336
21337+22337+24337+24338+25338+22338+21338
21339+22339+24339+24340+25340+22340+21340
21341+22341+24341+24342+25342+22342+21342
21343+22343+24343+24344+25344+22344+21344
21345+22345+24345+24346+25346+22346+21346
21347+22347+24347+24348+25348+22348+21348
21349+22349+24349+24350+25350+22350+21350
21351+22351+24351+24352+25352+22352+21352
21353+22353+24353+24354+25354+22354+21354
21355+22355+24355+24356+25356+22356+21356
21357+22357+24357+24358+25358+22358+21358
21359+22359+24359+24360+25360+22360+21360
21361+22361+24361+24362+25362+22362+21362
21363+22363+24363+24364+25364+22364+21364
21365+22365+24365+24366+25366+22366+21366
21367+22367+24367+24368+25368+22368+21368
21369+22369+24369+24370+25370+22370+21370
21371+22371+24371+24372+25372+22372+21372
21373+22373+24373+24374+25374+22374+21374
21375+22375+24375+24376+25376+22376+21376
21377+22377+24377+24378+25378+22378+21378
21379+22379+24379+24380+25380+22380+21380
21381+22381+24381+24382+25382+22382+21382
21383+22383+24383+24384+25384+22384+21384
21385+22385+24385+24386+23386+22386+21386
21387+22387+24387+24388+23388+22388+21388
21389+22389+24389+24390+23390+22390+21390
21391+22391+24391+24392+23392+22392+21392
21393+22393+24393+24394+23394+22394+21394
21395+22395+24395+24396+23396+22396+21396
21397+22397+24397+24398+23398+22398+21398
21399+22399+24399+24400+23400+22400+21400
21401+22401+24401+24402+23402+22402+21402
21403+22403+24403+24404+23404+22404+21404
21405+22405+24405+24406+23406+22406+21406
21407+22407+24407+24408+23408+22408+21408
21409+22409+24409+24410+23410+22410+21410
21411+22411+24411+24412+23412+22412+21412
21413+22413+24413+24414+23414+22414+21414
21415+22415+24415+24416+23416+22416+21416
21417+22417+24417+24418+23418+22418+21418
21419+22419+24419+24420+23420+22420+21420
21421+22421+24421+24422+23422+22422+21422
21423+22423+24423+24424+23424+22424+21424
21425+22425+24425+24426+23426+22426+21426
21427+22427+24427+24428+23428+22428+21428
21429+22429+24429+24430+23430+22430+21430
21431+22431+24431+24432+23432+22432+21432
21433+22433+24433+24434+23434+22434+21434
21435+22435+24435+24436+23436+22436+21436
21437+22437+24437+24438+23438+22438+21438
21439+22439+24439+24440+23440+22440+21440
21441+22441+24441+24442+23442+22442+21442
21443+22443+24443+24444+23444+22444+21444
21445+22445+24445+24446+23446+22446+21446
21447+22447+24447+24448+23448+22448+21448
21449+22449+24449+24450+23450+22450+21450
21451+22451+24451+24452+23452+22452+21452
21453+22453+24453+24454+23454+22454+21454
21455+22455+24455+24456+23456+22456+21456
21457+22457+24457+24458+23458+22458+21458
21459+22459+24459+24460+23460+22460+21460
21461+22461+24461+24462+23462+22462+21462
21463+22463+24463+24464+23464+22464+21464
21465+22465+24465+24466+23466+22466+21466
21467+22467+24467+24468+23468+22468+21468
21469+22469+24469+24470+23470+22470+21470
21471+22471+24471+24472+23472+22472+21472
21473+22473+24473+24474+23474+22474+21474
21475+22475+24475+24476+23476+22476+21476
21477+22477+24477+24478+23478+22478+21478
21479+22479+24479+24480+23480+22480+21480
21481+22481+24481+24482+23482+22482+21482
21483+22483+24483+24484+23484+22484+21484
21485+22485+24485+24486+23486+22486+21486
21487+22487+24487+24488+23488+22488+21488
21489+22489+24489+24490+23490+22490+21490
21491+22491+24491+24492+23492+22492+21492

21493+22493+24493+24494+23494+22494+21494
21495+22495+24495+24496+23496+22496+21496
21497+22497+24497+24498+23498+22498+21498
21499+22499+24499+24500+23500+22500+21500
21501+22501+24501+24502+23502+22502+21502
21503+22503+24503+24504+23504+22504+21504
21505+22505+24505+24506+23506+22506+21506
21507+22507+24507+24508+23508+22508+21508
21509+22509+24509+24510+23510+22510+21510
21511+22511+24511+24512+23512+22512+21512
21513+22513+24513+24514+23514+22514+21514
21515+22515+24515+24516+23516+22516+21516
21517+22517+24517+24518+23518+22518+21518
21519+22519+24519+24520+23520+22520+21520
21521+22521+24521+24522+23522+22522+21522
21523+22523+24523+24524+23524+22524+21524
21525+22525+24525+24526+23526+22526+21526
21527+22527+24527+24528+23528+22528+21528
21529+22529+24529+24530+23530+22530+21530
21531+22531+24531+24532+23532+22532+21532
21533+22533+24533+24534+23534+22534+21534
21535+22535+24535+24536+23536+22536+21536
21537+22537+24537+24538+23538+22538+21538
21539+22539+24539+24540+23540+22540+21540
21541+22541+24541+24542+23542+22542+21542
21543+22543+24543+24544+23544+22544+21544
21545+22545+24545+24546+23546+22546+21546
21547+22547+24547+24548+23548+22548+21548
21549+22549+24549+24550+23550+22550+21550
21551+22551+24551+24552+23552+22552+21552
21553+22553+24553+24554+23554+22554+21554
21555+22555+24555+24556+23556+22556+21556
21557+22557+24557+24558+23558+22558+21558
21559+22559+24559+24560+23560+22560+21560
21561+22561+24561+24562+23562+22562+21562
21563+22563+24563+24564+23564+22564+21564
21565+22565+24565+24566+23566+22566+21566
21567+22567+24567+24568+23568+22568+21568

S7+1 Sub-Surface Stock

8-car Double-ended sets

Formation: DM+M1+M2+MS+MS+M2+M1+DM

21323+22323+25384+24323+24324+25324+22324+21324
21327+22327+25386+24327+24328+25328+22328+21328

Notes
25xxx vehicles classified as M2D and fitted with de-icing equipment

Below: *The Circle, District and Hammersmith & City lines have been grouped together as they all use the recently introduced Bombardier S7 seven-vehicle sets. The Circle line is 17 miles (27km) in length with 36 stations, the District line is 40 miles (64km) with 60 stations, while the Hammersmith & City Line has 29 stations and is 15.8 miles (25.5km) in length. The S7 stock is based at Hammersmith depot. Each set has a top speed of 62mph (100km/h) and can accommodate 865 passengers. Seating is in the traditional longitudinal style. Each coach has three pairs of bi-parting sliding doors. Led by Driving Motor No. 21553, a S7 set approaches West Ham station.* **Antony Christie**

Right: *The S7 stock is formed of a Driving Motor at each end and five intermediate motor coaches. Three pairs of outside hung sliding doors allow a rapid entry/exit to the train allowing short station dwell times. On the outside of each vehicle is an electronic destination indicator. Vehicle No. 22523 is shown.* **CJM**

Left: *The interior of the S7 stock incorporates wide between vehicle open gangways, allowing a safer travelling experience as well as aiding the distribution of passengers. Passenger doors are driver controlled, rather than passenger operated. A high quality passenger information system is incorporated. The interior of vehicle No. 22523 is shown.* **CJM**

Right: *The front ends of the S7 stock incorporates a one-third width driving position with a central emergency door. Windscreen wipers are surprisingly fitted to this feature. Front end equipment consists of a destination indicator, train number display, dual headlights, marker and tail lights and an automatic coupling. DM No. 21540 leads a set at Dagenham East.*
Antony Christie

METROPOLITAN LINE

S8 Sub-Surface Stock

Builder: Bombardier, Derby
Years built: 2008-2012
Formation: DM+M1+M2+MS+MS+M2+M1+DM
Construction: Aluminium
Max speed: 62mph (100km/h)
Length: Driving - 57ft 2in (17.44m)
Intermediate - 50ft 6in (15.43m)
Width: 9ft 5in (2.92m)

Height: 12ft 0in (3.68m)
Gangway: Emergency end doors
Seating: Total 264
DM-34, M1-34, M2-34, MS-23
Doors: Sliding bi-parting
Traction equipment: 4 x Bombardier MJB20093 of 87hp (65kW) on each power car

8-car Double-ended sets

Formation: DM+M1+M2+MS+MS+M2+M1+DM

21001+22001+23001+24001+24002+25002+22002+21002
21003+22003+23003+24003+24004+25004+22004+21004
21005+22005+23005+24005+24006+25006+22006+21006
21007+22007+23007+24007+24008+25008+22008+21008
21009+22009+23009+24009+24010+25010+22010+21010
21011+22011+23011+24011+24012+25012+22012+21012
21013+22013+23013+24013+24014+25014+22014+21014
21015+22015+23015+24015+24016+25016+22016+21016
21017+22017+23017+24017+24018+25018+22018+21018
21019+22019+23019+24019+24020+25020+22020+21020
21021+22021+23021+24021+24022+25022+22022+21022
21023+22023+23023+24023+24024+25024+22024+21024
21025+22025+23025+24025+24026+25026+22026+21026
21027+22027+23027+24027+24028+25028+22028+21028
21029+22029+23029+24029+24030+25030+22030+21030
21031+22031+23031+24031+24032+25032+22032+21032
21033+22033+23033+24033+24034+25034+22034+21034
21035+22035+23035+24035+24036+25036+22036+21036
21037+22037+23037+24037+24038+25038+22038+21038
21039+22039+23039+24039+24040+25040+22040+21040
21041+22041+23041+24041+24042+25042+22042+21042
21043+22043+23043+24043+24044+25044+22044+21044
21045+22045+23045+24045+24046+25046+22046+21046
21047+22047+23047+24047+24048+25048+22048+21048
21049+22049+23049+24049+24050+25050+22050+21050
21051+22051+23051+24051+24052+25052+22052+21052
21053+22053+23053+24053+24054+25054+22054+21054
21055+22055+23055+24055+24056+25056+22056+21056
21057+22057+23057+24057+24058+23058+22058+21058
21059+22059+23059+24059+24060+23060+22060+21060
21061+22061+23061+24061+24062+23062+22062+21062
21063+22063+23063+24063+24064+23064+22064+21064
21065+22065+23065+24065+24066+23066+22066+21066
21067+22067+23067+24067+24068+23068+22068+21068
21069+22069+23069+24069+24070+23070+22070+21070
21071+22071+23071+24071+24072+23072+22072+21072
21073+22073+23073+24073+24074+23074+22074+21074
21075+22075+23075+24075+24076+23076+22076+21076
21077+22077+23077+24077+24078+23078+22078+21078
21079+22079+23079+24079+24080+23080+22080+21080
21081+22081+23081+24081+24082+23082+22082+21082
21083+22083+23083+24083+24084+23084+22084+21084
21085+22085+23085+24085+24086+23086+22086+21086
21087+22087+23087+24087+24088+23088+22088+21088
21089+22089+23089+24089+24090+23090+22090+21090
21091+22091+23091+24091+24092+23092+22092+21092
21093+22093+23093+24093+24094+23094+22094+21094
21095+22095+23095+24095+24096+23096+22096+21096
21097+22097+23097+24097+24098+23098+22098+21098
21099+22099+23099+24099+24100+23100+22100+21100
21101+22101+23101+24101+24102+23102+22102+21102
21103+22103+23103+24103+24104+23104+22104+21104
21105+22105+23105+24105+24106+23106+22106+21106
21107+22107+23107+24107+24108+23108+22108+21108
21109+22109+23109+24109+24110+23110+22110+21110
21111+22111+23111+24111+24112+23112+22112+21112
21113+22113+23113+24113+24114+23114+22114+21114
21115+22115+23115+24115+24116+23116+22116+21116

Vehicle named
21100 *Tim O'Toole CBE*

Notes
25xxx vehicles classified as M2D and fitted with de-icing equipment

Left: *Looking almost identical to the S7 stock, is the fleet of 58 eight-car S8 sets used on the Metropolitan Line. This fleet was built by Bombardier Transportation at Derby Litchurch Lane Works. These sets operate over the 42 miles (67km) 34 station route between Chesham/Amersham/Watford and Uxbridge through central London to Aldgate. Led by DM No. 21111 an S8 set passes Preston Road.* **Antony Christie**

Above: *An interesting comparison between tube and surface stock operating on London Underground. On the left is a Piccadilly Line 1973 unit, while on the right is a S8 working on the Metropolitan Line.* **Antony Christie**

Right: *The S8 stock has a mix of group and longitudinal seating, due to the length of the journeys undertaken, this sees each set seating 264. Intermediate motor No. 22031 is shown.* **Antony Christie**

With Driving Motor 21116 leading an S8 set is seen arriving at North Harrow. The DM vehicles of S8 stock seat 34. **CJM**

SERVICE STOCK

Former Passenger Stock

Rail Adhesion Train (RAT)

A60 stock
5110+6110+6036+6111+5111
D78 stock
7010+8123+17010+8010+7123

7040+8107+17040+8040+7107

Above: *London Underground surface lines are faced with the annual problem of leaf fall, to combat this a small fleet of Rail Adhesion Trains (RATs) are operated. For the 2018 season a recently converted five-car set of former D stock was introduced and operated on the Metropolitan and District lines. On 29 October 2018, one train, led by driving car 7040, is seen passing North Harrow. The inset image shows the treatment coach No. 17040. Both:* **CJM**

Track Recording Train

1960, 1967, 1972 and 1973 Tube stock
L132 (3901)+TRC666 (514)+L133 (3905)

3213+4213+3178 - For conversion into new inspection train
3079+4313+3313 - For conversion into new inspection train

Rail Adhesion (Sandite) and Pilot Stock

1956 and 1962 Stock
1406+2682+9125+1681+1682+9577+2406+1407 - Ued for Sandite and adhesion operations
1570+9691+2440+9441+1441 - Used for Sandite and adhesion operations
1560+2460+9561+1561 - Used as Pilot set

Filming Train
(at Aldwych)

1972 Stock
3229+4229+4329+3329

Locomotives
Schoma/Clayton

1	Diesel Hydraulic	Britta Lotta
2	Battery/Electric	Nikki
3	Diesel Hydraulic	Claire
4	Battery/Electric	Pam
5	Battery/Electric	Sophie
6	Battery/Electric	Denise
7	Battery/Electric	Annemarie
8	Battery/Electric	Emma
9	Diesel Hydraulic	Debora
10	Battery/Electric	Clementine
11	Battery/Electric	Joan
12	Diesel Hydraulic	Melanie
13	Battery/Electric	Michele
14	Battery/Electric	Carol

Track Machines

C623	7.5t crane
C624	7.5t crane
C625	7.5t crane
C626	7.5t crane
TRM627	Track relaying crane
TRM628	Track relaying crane
TMM771	Plasser 07-16 Universal
TMM772	Plasser 07-16 Universal
TMM773	Plasser 07-16 Universal
TMM774	Plasser 08-275
TMM775	Matisa B45UE (99 70 9128 003-9)
TMM776	Matisa B45UE (99 70 9128 004-7)

Battery / Electric

L15	69015, 97015, 97715
L16§	69016, 97016 - Seltrac equipped
L17§	69017, 97017 - Seltrac equipped
L18§	69018. 97018 - Seltrac equipped
L19§	69019, 97019 - Seltrac equipped
L20	69020, 97020 - Seltrac equipped
L21	64021, 97021 - Seltrac equipped
L22§	64022, 97022, 97722
L23§	64023, 97023
L24§	64024, 97024
L25§	64025, 97025
L26§	64026, 97026
L27§	64027, 97027 - Victoria line ATP equipped
L28§	64028, 97028 - Victoria line ATP equipped
L29§	64029, 97029 - Victoria line ATP equipped
L30§	64030, 97030 - Victoria line ATP equipped
L31§	64031, 97031 - Victoria line ATP equipped
L32§	64032, 97032, 97732 - Victoria line ATP equipped
L44§	73044, 97044 - Seltrac equipped
L45§	73045, 97045 - Seltrac equipped
L46§	73046, 97046 - Seltrac equipped
L47	73047, 97047 - Seltrac equipped
L48	73048, 97048 - Seltrac equipped
L49§	73049, 97049 - Seltrac equipped
L50§	73050, 97050 - Seltrac equipped
L51§	73051, 97051, 97751 - Seltrac equipped
L52	73052, 97052, 97752 - Seltrac equipped
L53§	73053, 97053, 97753 - Seltrac equipped
L54	73054, 97054 - Seltrac equipped

§ - Refurbished

Above: *To power engineering works trains on both tube and surface lines a fleet of battery/electric locos are maintained. No. L32 is captured during a night engineering run at Moorgate.* **Jamie Squibbs**

Transport for London Croydon Tramlink

Contact details as London Underground.

Bombardier *Flexity Swift* CR4000

Train Length: 98ft 9in (30.1m)
Width: 8ft 7in (2.65m)
Power Supply: 750V dc overhead
Seating: 70
Horsepower: 643hp (480kW)
Electrical Equipment: Bombardier

2530	2533	2536	2539	2542	2545	2548	2551§	§ Stored
2531	2534	2537	2540	2543	2546	2549	2552	
2532	2535	2538	2541	2544	2547	2550	2553	

Name applied

2535	***Stephen Parascandolo 1980-2007***

Left: *The Croydon Tramlink, operated by Transport for London and connecting Wimbledon with Croydon, Beckenham Junction, Elmers End and New Addington, is operated by two fleets of trams, the original Bombardier 'Flexity Swift' CR4000 and Stadler 'Variobahn' vehicles. Currently 23 Flexity Swift vehicles are in service, No. 2542 is seen at Arena.* **Antony Christie**

Above: *The Croydon Tramlink network operates with street running sections and dedicated rights of way, some of which were former railway routes. Original tram No. 2530 with a No. 3 service bound for Wimbledon is seen on a dedicated section near Lloyd Park.* **Antony Christie**

Stadler *Variobahn*

Train Length: 106ft 2½in (32.37m)
Width: 8ft 7in (2.65m)
Power Supply: 750V dc overhead
Seating: 70
Horsepower: 650hp (483kW)
Electrical Equipment: Stadler

2554	2556	2558	2560	2562	2564
2555	2557	2559	2561	2563	2565

Right: *By 2011 passenger growth on the Croydon tram system was such that extra trams were needed. This came in the form of an eventual fleet of 12 Stadler 'Variobahn' five-section vehicles, numbered in the series 2554-2565. Showing the design differences, 'Flexity' No. 2535 and 'Variobahn' No. 2559, pose side by side at Sandilands.* **Antony Christie**

Below: *The Stadler trams are slightly longer at 106ft 2½in than the original Bombardier products but the seating is the same at 70. No. 2560 is seen forming a Beckingham Junction service at Arena.* **Antony Christie**

Below: *The Croydon Tramlink operates full street running through Croydon town centre, sharing space with road vehicle and pedestrians, this includes area outside West Croydon and East Croydon main line stations. Stadler 'Variobahn' No. 2563 is captured approaching East Croydon station with a service to Elmers End.* **Antony Christie**

Transport for London Docklands Light Railway

Operated by KeolisAmey Docklands for Transport for London under contract until 2021.

Class B90 (twin)

Train Length: 94ft 5in (28.80m)
Width: 8ft 7in (2.65m)
Power Supply: 750V dc third rail
Seating: 52 + 4 tip-up
Horsepower: 375hp (280kW)
Electrical Equipment: Brush

22	24	26	28	30	32	34	36	38	40	42	44
23	25	27	29	31	33	35	37	39	41	43	

Left: *Docklands Light Railway, operated by Transport for London, currently operates four different series of trams. The B90 (twin) sets, numbered 22-44, were built by BN in Bruges, Belgium in 1991. The design seats 52 and all sets currently carry standard DLR red livery, with grey passenger doors and a black front end. Set no. 23 is seen passing the depot at Poplar.* **Antony Christie**

Below: *Since its original opening, the passenger growth on DLR has been massive, mainly attributable by the redevelopment of the former London Docklands area and opening many new businesses. The DLR network has also hugely expanded from its original system. Set No. 23 leads a three unit (six-car) train at East India.* **Antony Christie**

Class B92 (twin)

Train Length: 94ft 5in (28.80m)
Width: 8ft 7in (2.65m)
Power Supply: 750V dc third rail
Seating: 54 + 4 tip-up
Horsepower: 375hp (280kW)
Electrical Equipment: Brush

45	49	53	57	61	65	69	73	77	81	85	89
46	50	54	58	62	66	70	74	78	82	86	90
47	51	55	59	63	67	71	75	79	83	87	91
48	52	56	60	64	68	72	76	80	84	88	

Right: *In 1993 BN of Bruges, Belgium commissioned a fleet of 47 B92 twin cars, very similar in appearance to the B90s, but had seating for 54 plus two fold down seats. All DLR vehicles have two pairs of bi-parting sliding doors on each side of each vehicle. No, 62 is seen calling at Royal Victoria.* **Antony Christie**

Left: *DLR services usually operate as either two or three vehicle trains, giving either four or six passenger vehicles, giving seating for between 108 and 162, but with space for around three times that number to stand. Set No. 60 leads a double set formation at Gallions Reach.* **Antony Christie**

Class B2K (twin)

Train Length: 94ft 5in (28.80m)
Width: 8ft 7in (2.65m)
Power Supply: 750V dc third rail
Seating: 52 + 4 tip-up
Horsepower: 375hp (280kW)
Electrical Equipment: Brush

01	03	05	07	09	11	13	15	92	94	96	98
02	04	06	08	10	12	14	16	93	95	97	99

Right: *During 2002-2003 the B2K sets were delivered, these came from the now Bombardier plant in Bruges. Numbering was from 92-99 and then used the vacant positions of 01-16, replicating the numbers used by the original trams introduced in 1987. Set No. 97 leads a double set under the TfL cable car at West Silverton.* **Antony Christie**

Class B07 (twin)

Train Length: 94ft 5in (28.80m)
Width: 8ft 7in (2.65m)
Power Supply: 750V dc third rail
Seating: 52 + 4 tip-up
Horsepower: 375hp (280kW)
Electrical Equipment: Bombardier

101	106	111	116	121	126	131	136	141	146	151
102	107	112	117	122	127	132	137	142	147	152
103	108	113	118	123	128	133	138	143	148	153
104	109	114	119	124	129	134	139	144	149	154
105	110	115	120	125	130	135	140	145	150	155

Left: *Currently the most modern set of trams working on the Docklands Light Railway, emerged between 2008-2010 when Bombardier built a fleet of 55 B07 vehicles. These are of a slightly revised design, but again provide seating for 52 in each twin vehicle set. A six vehicle (three unit) train is seen at South Quay formed of sets Nos. 120, 151 and 127.* **Antony Christie**

Right: *The Docklands Railway operates under Automatic Train Operation at all times, with no driver being positioned on the train. However, a member of staff travels on all trains and is able to take manual control if required. A two set formation, led by No. 113, calls at Westferry.* **Antony Christie**

Left: *With much of the Docklands Light Railway built on bridges and new structures, some interesting pictures can be obtained in some locations. This is a view recorded at East India and shows a three set formation led by No. 129.* **Antony Christie**

Emirates Air Line
(Thames Cable Car) Transport for London

The Emirates Air Line or Thames Cable Car is a connection over the River Thames from Greenwich to the Royal Docks. The 1km line is operated by a fleet of 34 10-seat 'gondolas', and the end-to-end journey takes between 5 and 10 minutes depending on the speed of the service.

01	05	09	13	17	21	25	29	33
02	06	10	14	18	22	26	30	34
03	07	11	15	19	23	27	31	
04	08	12	16	20	24	28	32	

Right and below: *Perhaps not strictly 'light Rail' but a Transport for London service which is an impressive and interesting way to cross the London Docklands area - Thames Cable Car, operated as the Emirates Air Line, uses 34 10-seat gondolas providing a non-stop service between Greenwich Peninsula and Royal Docks. The vehicles are numbered, but do not operate in numerical order, some are removed each day for maintenance. The view right looks towards Royal Docks station. The image below, shows a close up of one of the gondolas No. 25.*
CJM / Antony Christie

Blackpool Tramway

Address: ✉ Blackpool Transport, Rigby Road, Blackpool, FY1 5DD
jean.cox@blackpooltransport.com
✆ 01253 473001 ⓘ www.blackpooltrams.info

Blackpool Tramway is operated by Blackpool Transport.

Flexity 2

Train Length: 105ft 9in (32.23m)
Width: 8ft 8in (2.65m)
Power Supply: 600V dc overhead
Seating: 74 + 148 standing
Horsepower: 4 x 160hp (120kW) three phase TMs
Electrical Equipment: Bombardier

001	003	005	007	009	011	013	015	017
002	004	006	008	010	012	014	016	018

Names applied

002	*Alderman E E Wynne*
007	*Alan Whitbread*

Left: *Originally opening in 1885, the Blackpool Tramway operates 11 miles (18km) from Starr Gate in the south to Fleetwood Ferry in the north, with 38 stops. The core passenger fleet consists of 18 Bombardier Flexity 2 five-section trams introduced in 2010-2017. Vehicle No. 005 is illustrated.* **Antony Christie**

Right: *When the Blackpool system was modernised in 2009-2010 a new depot was built at Starr Gate at the south end of the line to house and maintain the fleet. The old depot at Rigby Road is still retained to maintain the Heritage Fleet. Carrying advertising livery, Flexity 2 No. 014 is seen along the sea front.* **CJM**

Left: *The interior of the Bombardier Flexity 2 trams is of a high standard, using 2+2 seating with large amounts of standing room. Passenger access is by one sliding plug door on each end car, and a double leaf pair of sliding plug doors on the attached vehicles. The middle vehicle does not have external doors. Access to the drivers cab is by way of the passenger saloon.* **CJM**

Heritage Fleet

40	Fleetwood Box	648	Centenary	717	Balloon
66	Bolton Tram	680	Railcoach	718	Balloon
147	Standard	700	Balloon	719	Balloon
600	Boat	701	Balloon	723	Balloon
621	Brush	711	Balloon	733+734	Twin
631	Brush	713	Balloon	736	Illuminated (Frigate)
642	Centenary	715	Balloon	737	Illuminated (Boat)

Right: *When modernisation of the Blackpool Tramway was undertaken, agreement was reached to retain a number of Heritage Vehicles at Rigby Road depot and use these on special days as well as during the illumination events. The selection of vehicles are maintained to a very high standard. In this view we see 'Boat Car' No. 600.* **Richard Hargreaves**

Below: *Restored to the pleasing Blackpool Corporation cream and green livery, Brush single deck car No. 631 stands along the sea front.* **Richard Hargreaves**

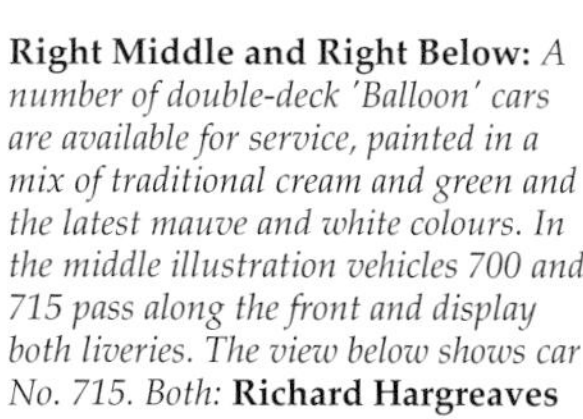

Right Middle and Right Below: *A number of double-deck 'Balloon' cars are available for service, painted in a mix of traditional cream and green and the latest mauve and white colours. In the middle illustration vehicles 700 and 715 pass along the front and display both liveries. The view below shows car No. 715. Both:* **Richard Hargreaves**

Edinburgh Tramway

Address: ✉ 55 Annandale Street, Edinburgh, EH7 4AZ

customer@edinburghtrams.com ✆ 0131 475 0177 ⓘhttp://edinburghtrams.com

CAF 7-section

Train Length: 140ft 5in (42.8m)	*Seating: 78 + 170 standing*
Width: 8ft 7in (2.65m)	*Horsepower: 1,287hp (960kW)*
Power Supply: 750V dc overhead	*Electrical Equipment: CAF*

251	255	259	263	267	271	275
252	256	260	264	268	272	276
253	257	261	265	269	273	277
254	258	262	266	270	274	

Left: *The capital of Scotland, Edinburgh returned to tram operation in the city in 2014, when the first phase of a much larger projected system opened between Edinburgh Airport and Edinburgh city centre, close to Edinburgh Waverley station. A fleet of 27 seven section CAF Urbos 3 trams were ordered, way too many for the present system, but will cover route expansion. The lines depot is located at Gogarburn at the Airport end of the system, where this view was recorded.* **Antony Christie**

Below: *The system operates on both segregated and street running. Each tram has seating for 78, with high quality leather covered seats in the 2+2 style. Tram No. 276 is seen near Edinburgh Haymarket.* **Antony Christie**

Above: *The Edinburgh tram fleet is finished in a white and Edinburgh Transport maroon livery, however in 2018 a major advertising contract was let and many trams now carry C R Smith advertising (an Edinburgh-based window and door company). Tram 271 is seen at Haymarket carrying Edinburgh Park branding.* **Antony Christie**

Below: *The tram system between Edinburgh Airport and the city centre operates every 7-10 minutes from early morning until late at night and is well used by the public. It offers a quick and efficient transport mode and interchanges with ScotRail rail services are provided at several stations. Trams 269 and 270 pass at Edinburgh Park.* **Antony Christie**

Glasgow Subway

Address: ✉ SPT, Consort House, 12 West George Street, Glasgow, G2 1HN
enquiry@spt.co.uk ✆ 0141 332 6811 ⓘ www.spt.co.uk

Glasgow Subway is operated by Strathclyde Partnership for Transport (SPT).
Gauge: 4ft (1219mm)

Single Power Cars

Length: 42ft 2in (12.81m) *Seating: 36S*
Width: 7ft 7in (2.34m) *Horsepower: 190hp (142.4kW)*
Power Supply: 600V dc third rail *Electrical Equipment: GEC*

101	104	107	110	113	116	119	122(S)	125	128	131
102	105	108	111	114	117	120	123	126	129	132
103	106	109	112	115	118	121	124	127	130	133

Trailer Cars

Length: 41ft 6in (12.70m) *Seating: 40S*
Width: 7ft 7in (2.34m)

201	202	203	204	205	206	207	208

Right: *Often known as 'The Clockwork Orange', the Glasgow Subway is a circular line below Glasgow City, with an outer and inner circle running in opposite directions. Currently the service is operated by a fleet of 33 power cars and eight trailers, but these are to be replaced with new trains in 2019-2020. Painted in orange livery, car No. 119 leads a train at Shields Road.* **Antony Christie**

Below: *Passenger accommodation is provided for 36 in driving cars and 40 in trailers, all set out in the longitudinal style. Passenger access is by two pairs of sliding doors on each side of each vehicle which are crew controlled. Lots of standing room is also provided as these trains can get very busy in peak periods.* **Antony Christie**

Above: *In 2016 driving car No. 101 was painted in heritage carmine and cream colours to mark the 120th anniversary of the line. The car is seen at Partick.* **Antony Christie**

Left: *The eight intermediate trailer vehicles were built after the main build and introduced in 1982 to cope with high passenger demand. Trailer No. 208 is illustrated, showing a rather interesting orange and grey livery style.* **Antony Christie**

Stadler Metro Sets

Train Length: 128ft 9in (39.24m) *Height: 8ft 8in (2.65m)*
Width: 7ft 7in (2.34m) *Seating: 104S + 6 folding, standing for 199S*

New 4-car articulated sets under construction and delivery, eventually will operate under Automatic Train Operation following total route modernisation.

001	003	005	007	009	011	013	015	017
002	004	006	008	010	012	014	016	

Right: *In 2016 Strathclyde Partnership for Transport ordered 17 new Stadler-built four vehicle articulated trains for the line, to be introduced in 2020-2021 and will operate under Automatic Train Operation reducing headways and increasing the number of trains. The first of the new trains was shown off at Innotrans held in Berlin in September 2018. The narrow 4ft gauge train is seen on display mounted on standard gauge 'dollies'. A driving cab is provided at just one end of each train, with an under-seat stowed slave cab at the other. Full height end emergency doors are provided.* **CJM**

Above Left: *The two intermediate vehicles of the new four-vehicle sets have bogies at only their inner ends, the outer end (illustrated) is suspended from the adjoining driving car which has two conventional two-axle bogies. Two pairs of bi-parting sliding doors are provided on driving cars while one pair of bi-parting doors are provided on intermediate coaches.* **CJM**

Above Right: *Vehicle interiors again use the longitudinal seating style, with seating for 104 on a four-car set, room exists for 199 standing passengers. Wide open gangways exist between vehicles.* **CJM**

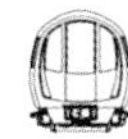

Below and Right: *Train configuration, showing disabled seating positions in both driving cars on left side in direction of travel.* **Stadler**

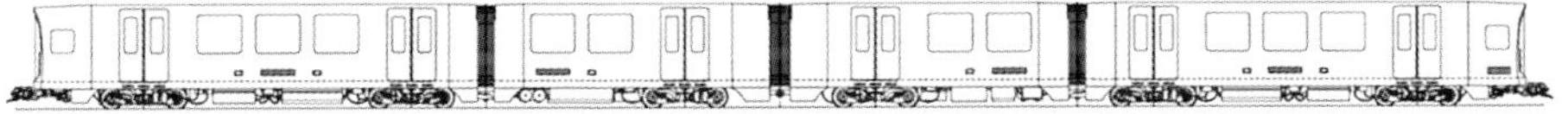

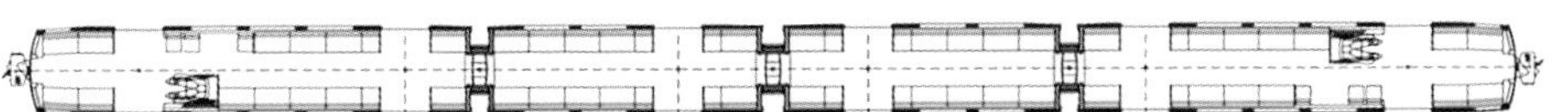

Manchester Metrolink

Address: ✉ Greater Manchester PTE, 2 Piccadilly Gardens, Manchester, M1 3BG
RATP Metrolink, Metrolink House, Queens Road, Manchester, M8 ORY
customerservices@metrolink.co.uk ✆ 0161 205 2000 ⓘ www.metrolink.co.uk

Metrolink is operated for GMPTE by Keolis Amey.

M5000 stock

Train Length: 93ft 1in (28.4m)
Width: 8ft 7in (2.65m)
Power Supply: 750V dc overhead
Seating: 52 + 8 tip-up
Horsepower: 643hp (480kW)
Electrical Equipment: Bombardier

3001	3015	3029	3043	3057	3071	3085	3099	3113	3127	3141
3002	3016	3030	3044	3058	3072	3086	3100	3114	3128	3142
3003	3017	3031	3045	3059	3073	3087	3101	3115	3129	3143
3004	3018	3032	3046	3060	3074	3088	3102	3116	3130	3144
3005	3019	3033	3047	3061	3075	3089	3103	3117	3131	3145
3006	3020	3034	3048	3062	3076	3090*	3104	3118	3132	3136
3007	3021	3035	3049	3063	3077	3091	3105	3119	3133	3147
3008	3022	3036	3050	3064	3078	3092	3106	3120	3134	
3009	3023	3037	3051	3065	3079	3093	3107	3121	3135	
3010	3024	3038	3052	3066	3080	3094	3108	3122	3136	
3011	3025	3039	3053	3067	3081	3095	3109	3123	3137	
3012	3026	3040	3054	3068	3082	3096	3110	3124	3138	
3013	3027	3041	3055	3069	3083	3097	3111	3125	3139	
3014	3028	3042	3056	3070	3084	3098	3112	3126	3140	

Names applied

3022	*The Spirit of Manchester*
3098	*Gracie Fields*

* Carries Gold 'Team GB' livery

Trams 3121-3147 on order

Left: *Outside London, the largest tramway system in the UK is in Manchester, where Metrolink operates a fleet of 120 two-section Bombardier Flexity Swift vehicles. An additional 27 are on order for delivery in 2019-2020. Nos. 3106 and 3097 are seen working through the city centre.* **Antony Christie**

Below: *Each car of the two section trams has two pairs of sliding doors, and seating is provided for between 52 and 60 depending on tram configuration. No. 3065 with seating for 52 is illustrated.* **Antony Christie**

Right: *From its original short system, by 2019 Manchester Metrolink has 62 miles of railway, 7 lines and 93 stations. In 2018 passenger figures were 41.2 million. The system operates as a mix of street running and dedicated tram tracks. Trains either operate as single or double units giving two or four-car length trains. Set No. 3037 is seen from its B car at the Eccles terminal.*
Antony Christie

Left: *A twin set formation with tram No. 3034 nearest the camera is seen under the glazed roof at the rebuilt Manchester Victoria station.* **Antony Christie**

Below: *The area through Manchester City Centre is all street running, with pedestrians, road traffic and trams all sharing the right of way, very few problems exist and the system runs very well providing the major inner-city travelling experience. Tram No. 3025 pulls onto its own right of way close to the Manchester Arndale shopping centre.*
Antony Christie

West Midlands Metro

Address: ✉ Travel West Midlands, PO Box 3565, Birmingham, B1 3JR
info@travelmetro.co.uk ✆ 0121 254 7272 ⓘ www.travelmetro.co.uk

Urbos 3

Train Length: 108ft 3in (29m)
Width: 8ft 8in (2.65m)
Power Supply: 750V dc overhead
Seating: 54 + 156 standing
Horsepower: 1,320hp (960kW)
Builder: CAF

17	26	35§	*Angus Adams*
18§	27	36§	
19	28§	37	*Ozzy Osbourne*
20	29		
21§	30		
22	31§		
23	32		
24	33		
25	34		

§ Fitted with traction batteries

Tender out for between 18 and 32 new trams

T69 tram No. 16 retained at Midland Metro depot for engineering use

Above: *The West Midlands Metro operates from Birmingham city centre to Wolverhampton by way of a tram alignment on the former GW railway route. The line has a depot at Wednesbury where the current fleet of 21 CAF Urbos 3 trains are based. Tram No. 20 is seen at Wednesbury Parkway.* **CJM**

Left: *In summer 2018 a start was made at applying a new West Midlands blue livery to the tram fleet, as shown on Tram No. 31 at West Bromwich Central. A major extension to the tram system is now underway from the present terminal at Grand Central into the City centre.* **John Binch**

Right: *The CAF Urbos 3 trams used in the West Midlands seat 54 with room for around 156-160 standees. The layout uses a mix of longitudinal and group seats.* **CJM**

Below and Bottom: *Traction battery technology has advanced to such a level that it is now possible to power trams with on board batteries. CAF fitted tram No. 31 with a battery power system to allow it to operate without the requirement of overhead power lines. Trials established the system to be satisfactory and now the city extension will be built without overhead wire. In 2018-2019 a progressive work project is being undertaken at the depot to install traction batteries. Modified trams can be identified by an extra box on the roof of driving cars at the outer end, as shown on No. 36 at Black Lake. Modified trams also carry a Urbos Tram Lithium Battery logo on the bodyside, shown below.* **Antony Christie / CJM**

Nottingham Express Transit

Address: ✉ Transdev Tram UK Ltd, Garrick House, 74 Chiswick High Road, London, W4 1SY
Nottingham City Transport Ltd, Lower Parliament Street, Nottingham, NG1 1GG
info@thetram.net ✆ 0115 942 7777 ⓘ www.thetram.net

Incentro AT6/5

Train Length: 108ft 3in (29m)
Width: 7ft 9in (2.4m)
Power Supply: 750V dc overhead
Seating: 54 + 4 tip-up
Horsepower: 697hp (520kW)
Electrical Equipment: Bombardier

No.	Name
201	*Torvill and Dean*
202	*DH Lawrence*
203	*William 'Bendigo' Thompson*
204	*Erica Beardsmore*
205	*Lord Byron*
206	*Angela Alcock*
207	*Mavis Worthington*
208	*Dinah Minton*
209	*Sid Standard*
210	*Sir Jesse Boot*
211	*Robin Hood*
212	*William Booth*
213	*Mary Potter*
214	*Dennis McCarthy MBE*
215	*Brian Clough*

Citadis 302

Train Length: 104ft 11¾in (32m)
Width: 7ft 9in (2.4m)
Power Supply: 750V dc overhead
Seating: 58 + 6 tip-up
Horsepower: 644hp (480kW)
Builder: Alstom

No.	Name
216	*Dame Laura Knight*
217	*Carl Froch*
218	*Jim Taylor*
219	*Alan Sillitoe*
220	*Luisa Avanzado*
221	*Stephen Lowe*
222	*Michelle and Richard Daniels*
223	*Colin Slater MBE*
224	*Vicky McClure*
225	*Doug Scott CBE*
226	*Jimmy Sirrel & Jack Wheeler*
227	*Sir Peter Mansfield*
228	*Local Armed Forces Heroes*
229	*Viv Anderson MBE*
230	*George Green*
231	*Rebecca Adlington OBE*
232	*William Ivory*
233	*Ada Lovelace*
234	*George Africanus*
235	*David Clarke*
236	*Sat Bains*
237	*Stuart Broad*

Right: *The City of Nottingham commenced using modern trams in 2004, with the opening of the Nottingham Express Transit system. The original network has now been extended and currently operates a 20 mile system with 51 stops. Originally a fleet of 15 Bombardier Incentro AT6/5 trams were introduced. No. 201 is seen at Inham Road.* **Antony Christie**

Left: *Trams on the Nottingham system are based at a depot at Wilkinson Street, where all work is undertaken. The large facility can be clearly seen from passing trams. No. 203 is seen at Southchurch Lane. The Incentro trams seat 54, with room for around three times that number to stand.* **Antony Christie**

Right: *In 2013-2014 extra trams were needed for the Nottingham system and a fleet of 22 Alstom Citadis 302 trams were ordered. These five-section vehicles were slightly shorter than the original fleet, but seated 58. With their stylish European front end design the fleet settled down well and now share duties with the earlier delivery. No. 216* Dame Laura Knight *is illustrated at Wilford Village.* **Antony Christie**

Left: *Like most modern UK tram systems, the Nottingham system operates as a mix of dedicated and street running, with all platforms being of the low level design. No. 228 named* Local Armed Forces Heroes *is seen at Bramcote Lane.* **Antony Christie**

Right: *Alstom Citadis 302 interior, showing the 2+2 group seating layout, with wide gangways between vehicles, plenty of standing space is provided as is accommodation for disabled wheelchairs, prams and bicycles. A good passenger information system is also provided, providing tram stopping and route information.* **Antony Christie**

South Yorkshire SuperTram

Address: ✉ Stagecoach SuperTram, Nunnery Depot, Woodburn Road, Sheffield, S9 3LS

enquiries@supertram.com ✆ 0114 272 8282 ⓘ www.supertram.com

Six-axle Stock

Train Length: 113ft 6in (34.75m)	*Seating: 88 + 6 tip-up*
Width: 8ft 7in (2.65m)	*Horsepower: 800hp (596kW)*
Power Supply: 750V dc overhead	*Electrical Equipment: Siemens*

101	103	105	107	109	111	113	115	117	119	121	123	125
102	104	106	108	110	112	114	116	118	120	122	124	

Name applied

123	*Pete McKee*

Left: *The Yorkshire City of Sheffield is home of the South Yorkshire Supertram, a network of 18 miles (29km) with 48 stations over three lines which opened in March 1994. To operate the system, a fleet of 25 Siemens three-section trams were built, Nos. 101-125 based at Nunnery depot. No. 122 painted in Stagecoach Supertram livery is seen at the Sheffield station stop.* **CJM**

Below: *With accommodation for 88 seated passengers, these are some of the highest density trams in the UK. No. 112 is seen at Cathedral.* **CJM**

Above: *All of the South Yorkshire Supertram lines operate over a core Sheffield city centre section, with an intense service between Fitzalan Square and Cathedral. Tram No. 120 sports a special blue and cream livery, applied in 2010 to mark the 50th anniversary of the end of the original Sheffield tram system. The vehicle is seen departing from the city with a Halfway service.* **CJM**

Right Middle: *In 2018-2019 two trams sport a pink livery advertising the womans fashion business Pretty Little thing. Showing this livery, No. 111 is seen in the city centre.* **CJM**

Right Lower: *True street running, sharing space with road vehicles and pedestrians. Much of the line from the city centre to Herdings Park and Halfway operates in this way. No. 123 is seen at the White Lane stop.* **CJM**

Class 399 *CityLink*

Train Length: 122ft 0¾in (37.2m)
Width: 8ft 8½in (2.65m)
Power supply: 750V dc overhead (equipped for 25kV ac operation)
Power equipment: 6 x 145kW VEM traction motors
Seats (total/car): 88S, 22S/44S/22S

Number	Formation DMOSW+MOS+DMOSW	Depot	Livery	Owner	Operator	Name
399201 (201)*	999001+999101+999201	§	SST	SST	SST	
399202 (202)*	999002+999102+999202	§	SST	SST	SST	*Theo The Childrens Hospital Charity*
399203 (203)*	999003+999103+999203	§	SST	SST	SST	
399204 (204)*	999004+999104+999204	§	SST	SST	SST	
399205 (205)	999005+999105+999205	§	SST	SST	SST	
399206 (206)*	999006+999106+999206	§	SST	SST	SST	
399207 (207)	999007+999107+999207	§	SST	SST	SST	

* Authorised for TramTrain operation. § - Sheffield Nunnery SST - Sheffield Super Tram

Left: *With 'TT' displayed in the route indicator, Class 399 'TramTrain' No. 201 (399201) calls at the new low level platform at Rotherham Central with a service from Rotherham Parkgate to Sheffield Cathedral.* **CJM**

Below: *At present the TramTrains terminate at Sheffield Cathedral, using the track nearest to the Cathedral. At the launch of the service in October 2018, three trains per hour were operated in each direction, using trams fitted with modified ME1 tyre profiles. No. 201 (399201) is seen departing from the Cathedral stop.* **CJM**

Above: *At Rotherham Parkgate, an out of town retail park, a new tram-length low height platform has been built, on a short spur off the Network Rail line. On 1 November 2018, No. 203 (399203) awaits departure from the Rotherham Parkgate station bound for Cathedral.* **CJM**

Below: *Set No. 202 (399202) passes slowly through the standard height Network Rail platforms at Rotherham Central, approaching the low level TramTrain platform while working a service from Rotherham Parkgate to Sheffield Cathedral. The Network Rail TramTrain section is energised at 750V dc using the overhead system, as used in Sheffield city centre.* **CJM**

Tyne & Wear Metro

Address: ✉ Tyne & Wear Passenger Transport Executive (NEXUS), Nexus House, 33 St James Boulevard, Newcastle upon Tyne, NE1 4AX
enquiries@nexus.co.uk
✆ 0191 203 3333 ⓘ www.nexus.org.uk

Tyne & Wear Metro stock is allocated TOPS classification 994 for operation over Network Rail metals between Pelaw and South Hylton.

Six-axle Stock

Train Length: 91ft 3in (27.80m)	*Seating: 68*
Width: 8ft 7in (2.65m)	*Horsepower: 500hp (374kW)*
Power Supply: 1500V dc overhead	*Electrical Equipment: Siemens*

4001	4013	4025	4037	4049	4061	4073	4085
4002	4014	4026	4038	4050	4062	4074	4086
4003	4015	4027	4039	4051	4063	4075	4087
4004	4016	4028	4040	4052	4064	4076	4088
4005	4017	4029	4041	4053	4065	4077	4089
4006	4018	4030	4042	4054	4066	4078	4090
4007	4019	4031	4043	4055	4067	4079	
4008	4020	4032	4044	4056	4068	4080	
4009	4021	4033	4045	4057	4069	4081	
4010	4022	4034	4046	4058	4070	4082	
4011	4023	4035	4047	4059	4071	4083	
4012	4024	4036	4048	4060	4072	4084	

Name applied (inside)
4041 *Harry Cowans*

Tyne and Wear Metro sets are based at Gosforth depot, in 2019 a new depot will open at Howdon, to provide extra cover while Gosforth depot is modernised to cope with new stock. Howdon will also be a delivery point for new trains.

Below: *Opening in the mid 1970s, the oldest of the 'modern' UK light rail systems apart from London Transport, is the Tyne & Wear Metro, radiating from Newcastle. Today the system extends to two lines, covering 48.2 miles (77.5km) with 60 stations. A fleet of 90 twin Metro-Cammell built sets are the current motive power, but tenders are currently being submitted for new stock. Set No. 4064 is seen approaching Benton.* **Antony Christie**

Right: *The Tyne & Wear system operates over largely former 'heavy-rail' lines converted for light rail operation, with some new build lines. Trains usually operate as two twin-sets coupled together providing four carriages with seating for 136. Displaying the latest black and yellow livery, No. 4077 is illustrated at Fawdon on the Newcastle Airport branch.* **Antony Christie**

Left: *The operational headquarters of the Tyne & Wear Metro is at South Gosforth, where administrative offices and the fleets depot is located. Passing below the stations historic footbridge, set No. 4005 calls at South Gosforth station with a service bound for Newcastle Airport.* **Antony Christie**

Below: *Although the Tyne & Wear Metro is a UK light railway, it does not have street running and operates on a railway basis. Station platforms are of conventional height, set No. 4028 is recorded calling at Bank Foot station.* **Antony Christie**

■ Tyne & Wear Metro also operates three battery-electric shunting locomotives at South Gosforth, BL1-BL3, these are registered National Fleet numbers 97901, 97902 and 97903.

■ In 2018 five builders were invited to bid to build a fleet of new Tyne and Wear trams, the short list is Bombardier, CAF, Hitachi, Stadler and a consortium of Downer EDI Rail/China Rail. The winner will be announced at the end of 2019.

Dublin 'Luas' Trams

Trams returned to the streets of Dublin in 2004, and currently two lines operate with three batches of Alstom Citadis trams. Overhead power is provided at 750V dc. Seating on trams is for 70-72, with standing room for three times that number.

Alstom Citadis TGA301 five-section vehicles introduced 2002-03

3001	3005	3009	3013	3017	3021	3025
3002	3006	3010	3014	3018	3022	3026
3003	3007	3011	3015	3019	3023	
3004	3008	3012	3016	3020	3024	

Left: *In Dublin, Ireland a busy tram system operates, named Luas. The system operates as two lines, with four batches of trams in use, all supplied by Alstom of the Citadis type. A fleet of 26 3000 class sets operate on the red line, these are five-section (originally three-section) vehicles introduced in 2002-2004. No. 3010 is illustrated at Dublin Heuston.* **CJM**

Alstom Citadis TGA401 five-section vehicles introduced 2002-03

4001	4003	4005	4007	4009	4011	4013
4002	4004	4006	4008	4010	4012	4014

Left: *The second batch of trams to be introduced were the 4000 series, built as five-section units from new. These operate on the red line with a handful working on the green line. No. 4002 is seen pulling into the Museum stop on the red line.* **CJM**

Alstom Citadis TGA402 seven-section, vehicles introduced 2008-2010

5001	5005	5009	5013	5017	5021	5025
5002	5006	5010	5014	5018	5022	5026
5003	5007	5011	5015	5019	5023	
5004	5008	5012	5016	5020	5024	

To be extended to nine section vehicles from late 2019.

Left: *Between 2008-2010 a batch of 26 Citadis 402 seven-section trams were introduced to operate on the green line, being based at Sandyford depot. Although longer, these sets had less seats than the five section units, having a greater standing area, especially around door pockets. No. 5023 is shown at the late 2017 opened terminus of Broombridge.* **CJM**

Alstom Citadis TGA402 nine-section vehicles introduced 2017-2018

5027	5028	5029	5030	5031	5032	5033

Eight more nine-section trams to be ordered.

Above: *To cope with passenger growth and the opening of an extension of the green line through Dublin city centre, seven new Citadis 402 series trams were delivered in 2017-2018. These were nine-section units, some of the longest operating on any line. Technical issues saw many sets out of service in 2018, with limited peak hour service only reported. Nine-car set No. 5029 is illustrated at St Stephen's Green.* **CJM**

Right: *LUAS tram interior, showing the spacious accommodation with seats and large standing areas.* **CJM**

Great Orme Tramway

Address: ✉ Victoria Station, Church Walks, Llandudno, North Wales. LL30 2NB.
tramwayenquiries@conwy.gov.uk
✆ 01492 577 877 ⓘ www.greatormetramway.co.uk

The Great Orme Tramway operates between Victoria station in Llandudno and the summit of The Great Orme. The line is operated in two sections: Llandudno to Halfway and Halfway to Summit.

Single Bogie Cars

Built By: Hurst Nelson, Motherwell	*Seating: 48*
Introduced: 1902	*Speed: 5mph (8km/h)*
Power: Cable	*Gauge: 3ft 6in (1067mm)*

Lower section		Upper section	
4	*St Tudno*	6	*St Seiriol*
5	*St Silio*	7	*St Trillo*

Left: *Four tramcars of 1902 vintage operate on the Great Orme Tramway, working as two pairs on the 'upper' and 'lower' sections. Tram 7* St Trillo *on the upper section is seen approaching Halfway station from Summit. From Halfway station passengers will have to disembark and make a short walk to the other end of the station to catch the lower section tram for the remainder of their journey to Llandudno.* **CJM**

Hythe Pier Tramway

Address: ✉ The Pier, Prospect Place, Hythe, Southampton. SO45 6AU.
www.hytheferry.co.uk
✆ 023 8084 0722 ⓘ http://hytheferry.co.uk

The Hythe Pier Tramway operates along the pier in Hythe near Southampton and takes ferry boat passengers from the end of the pier on a 700 yard (640m) journey to the town. The line is electrified using the third rail system at 250V dc.

4-wheel locos

Built By: Brush	*Seating: Nil*
Introduced: 1917 as battery, now electric	*Speed: 10mph (16km/h)*
Power: 250V dc third rail	*Gauge: 2ft (610mm)*

1	**Works No. 16302**	2	**Works No. 16307**

Rolling stock
Four bogie passenger carriages, two fitted with remote driving controls
One four-wheel freight platform wagon, One oil carrying tank car

Left: *Two four-wheel electric locos are the motive power for the 700yard long Hythe Pier Tramway. No. 1, leading three carriages and a flat car for luggage arrives at Hythe Town.* **CJM**

Southend Pier Tramway

Address: ✉ Western Esplanade, Southend-on-Sea SS1 2EL
council@southend.gov.uk
✆ 01702 611214 ⓘ www.southend.gov.uk

Southend Pier Railway operates as a tourist attraction between the Shore Station and the Pier Head, a distance of 1.25m (2.01km). It is operated by two diesel-hydraulic locos and 12 passenger cars

Seven-vehicle sets

Built By: Severn Lamb Engineering	*Seating: Train - 200*
Introduced: 1986	*Speed: 10mph (16km/h)*
Power: Diesel	*Gauge: 3ft (914mm)*

A	***Sir John Betjeman***	B	***Sir William Heygate***

Right: *The Southend Pier Railway which operates 1.25miles (2.01km) between the Shore station and the Pier head is operated by two seven-vehicle trains, with a diesel loco at the pier head end and a cab car at the shore end. Train 'A' with diesel-hydraulic loco* Sir John Betjeman *is seen at the Pier Head station.* **CJM**

Volks Electric Railway

Address: ✉ Madeira Drive, Brighton and Hove BN2, UK
contact via website
✆ 01273 292718 ⓘ www.volkselectricrailway.co.uk

Volks Electric Railway operates along the sea front at Brighton between Aquarium to Black Rock, a distance of 1.02m (1.64km). It is electrified at 110V dc and currently has a fleet of seven electric passenger cars.

3	**40 seat open of 1892**
4	**40 seat open of 1892**
6	**40 seat open of 1901**
7	**40 seat open of 1901**
8	**40 seat open of 1901**
9	**40 seat open of 1910**
10	**40 seat open of 1926**

Right: *Volks Electric Railway which runs along the sea front in Brighton is technically the oldest electric railway, opening in 1883. Today, the line is operated over a shorter distance and currently a fleet of seven powered double-ended vehicles are in service, usually working in pairs. No. 7, a 40 seat open vehicle built in 1901 is seen departing from Aquarium.* **CJM**

Seaton Tramway

Address: ✉ Seaton Tramway, Harbour Road, Seaton, Devon. EX12 2NQ.
info@tram.co.uk
✆ 01297 20375 ⓘ www.tram.co.uk

The Seaton Tramway operates between Seaton and Colyton along the bank of the River Axe with one intermediate station at Colyford. It is a 2ft 9in (838 mm) narrow gauge electric tramway, 3 miles (4.8 km) in length. It operates over part of the former Seaton Branch line of the L&SWR (SR), which closed in March 1966. The tramway was established in 1970, and previously operated in Eastbourne between 1954 and 1969.

02	1952	Works vehicle
2	1964	Based on London Metropolitan Tramways Type A vehicle No. 14
4	1961	Based on Blackpool 'Open Boat' design
6	1954	Based on Bournemouth open topper design. Originally single decker in Llandudno
7	1958	Based on Bournemouth open topper design
8	1968	Based on Bournemouth open topper design, displays Bristol blue livery
9	2004	Hybrid design based on Plymouth and Blackburn trams
10	2006	Hybrid design based on Plymouth and Blackburn trams
11	2007	Based on Bournemouth open topper design, displays 'pink' charity livery
12	1966	Based on London 'Feltham' design
14	1904	Oldest tram built as Metropolitan Tramways Type A car No. 94 (originally standard gauge)
15	1988	Enclosed saloon, based on Isle of Man design and in Isle of Man livery
16	1921	Originally Bournemouth open top car No. 106
19	1909	Originally Exeter Tramways vehicle

Left: *Although not a tramway or Light Railway in the true sense, the Seaton Tramway which is operated as a visitor attraction, shows many thousands each year how tram transport operated. All but three of the trams were purpose built to replicate a real vehicle. Three trams (14, 16 and 19) are original tram bodies fitted to 2ft 9in (838mm) gauge trucks. No. 12 was built in 1966 and is based on the London Transport 'Feltham' design.* **CJM**

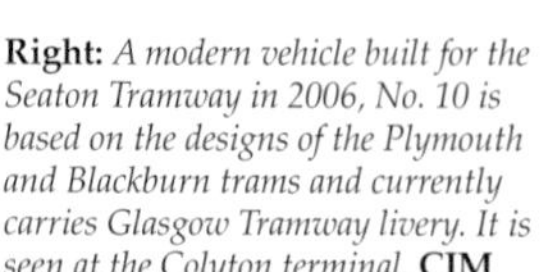
Right: *A modern vehicle built for the Seaton Tramway in 2006, No. 10 is based on the designs of the Plymouth and Blackburn trams and currently carries Glasgow Tramway livery. It is seen at the Colyton terminal.* **CJM**

Above: *Tram No. 8 is based on the style of a Bournemouth open top tram. This vehicle was constructed in 1968. It is currently painted in Bristol blue livery.* **CJM**

Right: *Always a very popular tram on the line is the 1964-built replica of a London Metropolitan Tramway Type 'A' tram. This demonstrates just how open these vehicles were to the motorman and upper deck passengers, who had no protection during inclement weather. No. 2 is seen arriving at the mid station Colyford.* **CJM**

Isle of Man Railways

Manx Electric Railway

The Manx Electric Railway is a 3ft (914mm)-gauge twin-track line which operates from Douglas Derby Castle to Ramsey, a distance of 17 miles (27.4km). It is energised at 550V dc using the overhead power collection system. The main car shops are located at Derby Castle. At Laxey a passenger interchange with the Snaefell Mountain Railway is provided. Trains usually operate only between March and October.

Power Cars

Number	Type	Builder	Year
1	Un-vestibuled saloon	G F Milnes	1893
2	Un-vestibuled saloon	G F Milnes	1893
5	Vestibuled 'Tunnel car'	G F Milnes	1894
6	Vestibuled 'Tunnel car'	G F Milnes	1894
7	Vestibuled 'Tunnel car'	G F Milnes	1894
9	Vestibuled 'Tunnel car'	G F Milnes	1894
14	Cross-bench open saloon	G F Milnes	1898
15 (S)	Cross-bench open saloon	G F Milnes	1898
16	Cross-bench open saloon	G F Milnes	1898
17 (S)	Cross-bench open saloon	G F Milnes	1898
18 (S)	Cross-bench open saloon	G F Milnes	1898
19	Winter saloon	G F Milnes	1899
20	Winter saloon	G F Milnes	1899
21	Winter saloon	G F Milnes	1899
22	Winter saloon	McArds/MER	1992*
23 (S)	Locomotive	MER Co	1900
25 (S)	Cross-bench open	G F Milnes	1893
26 (S)	Cross-bench open	G F Milnes	1893
27 (S)	Cross-bench open	G F Milnes	1893
28 (S)	Cross-bench open	ER&T Ltd	1904
29 (S)	Cross-bench open	ER&T Ltd	1904
30 (S)	Cross-bench open	ER&T Ltd	1904
31 (S)	Cross-bench open	ER&T Ltd	1904
32	Cross-bench 'Toastrack'	United Car	1906
33	Cross-bench 'Toastrack'	United Car	1906
34	Locomotive	IOM	1996

* rebuilt following fire damage - new body on old frame

Left: *The Isle of Man offers one of the most amazing transport experiences, with four different, very interesting 'railway' systems. The Manx Electric Railway, which operates 17 miles (27.4km) from Douglas Derby Castle to Ramsey via Laxey offers passengers the chance to ride on some of the oldest operational trams in the world. In this view, Tram No. 1, built in 1893 hauls trailer car No. 42, built in 1903, towards Laxey.* **CJM**

Below: *1906-built United Car Cross-bench 'Toastrack' No. 32, displaying Manx Electric Railway green and white colours is seen at Derby Castle.* **CJM**

Isle of Man Railways

Above: *Built by G F Milnes of Birkenhead in 1894 is Vestibuled 'Tunnel Car' No. 5, a regular performer on the line offering enclosed accommodation. In immaculate condition, as all the operational vehicles are, No. 5 is seen without a trailer at Laxey with a service bound for Ramsey.* **CJM**

Right Middle: *In 2018, No. 14 returned to service after some 30 plus years out of traffic and restoration by staff and volunteers at Derby Castle depot. Restored to maroon and white and carrying the legend Douglas and District Electric Railway, No. 14 is illustrated at Groudle.* **CJM**

Right Lower: *Built in 1899 by Milnes of Birkenhead is 'Winter Saloon' No. 19, so called as it provided enclosed accommodation for winter travel. No. 19 is viewed at Laxey hauling a trailer bound for Douglas Derby Castle.* **CJM**

Above: *In addition to the main workshop at Derby Castle, a smaller engineering facility exists at Laxey, where many of the more unusual vehicles can be found. Painted in Manx Electric Railway green and white, 1899-built Winter Saloon is seen inside the depot.* **CJM**

Left: *No. 34 is officially a locomotive, built in 1996 for the Snaefell Mountain Railway as a replica of No. 7 to mark the lines centenary. Now on the Manx Electric Railway the loco is out of use at Laxey Car Shed.* **CJM**

Below: *Built by the Manx Electric Railway in 1925 is loco No. 23, a centre cab vehicle with two fixed open wagons at either end. It is currently out of use at Laxey.* **CJM**

Trailer Cars

Number	Type	Builder	Year
36 (S)	Cross-bench	G F Milnes	1894
37 (S)	Cross-bench	G F Milnes	1894
40	Cross-bench	English Electric	1930
41	Cross-bench	English Electric	1930
42	Cross-bench	G F Milnes	1903
43 (S)	Cross-bench	G F Milnes	1903
44	Cross-bench	English Electric	1930
46	Cross-bench	G F Milnes	1899
47	Cross-bench	G F Milnes	1899
48	Cross-bench	G F Milnes	1899
49 (S)	Cross-bench	G F Milnes	1893
50 (S)	Cross-bench	G F Milnes	1893
51	Cross-bench	G F Milnes	1893
53 (S)	Cross-bench	G F Milnes	1893
54 (S)	Cross-bench	G F Milnes	1893
55 (S)	Cross-bench	ER&T Ltd	1904
56	Disabled persons	ER&T Ltd	1904*
57	Enclosed saloon	ER&T Ltd	1904
58	Enclosed saloon	ER&T Ltd	1904
59	Special/Directors saloon	G F Milnes	1895
60	Cross-bench	G F Milnes	1896
61	Cross-bench	United Electric	1906
62	Cross-bench	United Electric	1906

* Modified by MER 1995

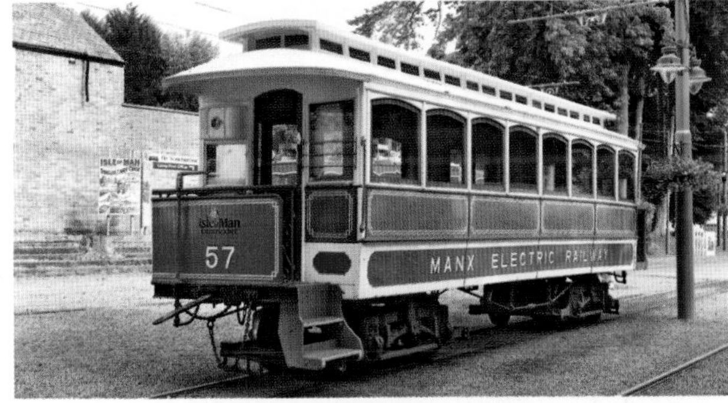

Right Upper: *To operate alongside the interesting fleet of power cars, is an equally amazing fleet of vintage trailer vehicles. No. 57 is a short wheelbase 'Enclosed Saloon' built by Electric Rail and Traction Ltd in 1904. It is currently restored to Manx Electric Railway varnished, red and white and is seen stabled at Laxey.* **CJM**

Right Middle: *In 1899 G F Milnes of Birkenhead built three Cross-Bench open trailers Nos. 46-48, these had hinged seating to enable passengers to face the direction of travel. No fixed sides were provided, but roller-shutters were installed to protect passengers during inclement weather. No. 48 is restored to the white and blue livery, and often operates with Tunnel Car No. 7 which is restored to the same livery. No. 48 is viewed at Derby Castle station.* **CJM**

Right Lower: *Provision is made for disabled travellers on the Manx Electric Railway, with a special lift fitted to Enclosed Saloon No. 56. The lift provides access for a wheelchair and stabling facilities are provided inside the vehicle.* **CJM**

Freight and Service Vehicles

Number	Type	Builder	Year
1	Tower wagon	G F Milnes	1894
3	Van	G F Milnes	1894
4	Travelling Post Office van	G F Milnes	1894
8	Open wagon	G F Milnes	1897
10	Open wagon	G F Milnes	1897
11	Van 6-ton	G F Milnes	1898
12	Van 6-ton	G F Milnes	1899
13	Van 5-ton	G F Milnes	1903
14	Van 5-ton	G F Milnes	1904
16	Mail van	MER	1908
21	Flat wagon	MER	1926
26	Freight trailer	G F Milnes	1918*
45	Flat wagon	G F Milnes	1899§
52	Flat wagon with work lift	G F Milnes	1893±
RF308	Tipper wagon	Hudson	1993■
13/24-4(S)	Tipper wagon	W G Allan	1997
13/24-5(S)	Tipper wagon	W G Allan	1997
13/24-6(S)	Tipper wagon	W G Allan	1997
7442/2	Trailer	Wickham	2014

* Rebuilt from frame of power car 10
§ Rebuilt from trailer passenger car 45 in 2004
± Rebuilt from passenger trailer 52 in 1947, lift fitted 2008
■ Former Channel Tunnel vehicle

Left Upper: *Although no freight traffic is now carried by the Manx Electric Railway, some of the original freight cars are restored and make occasional runs on the line to recreate the past. Open wagon No. 10, built in 1897 is seen stored inside Laxey car sheds.* **CJM**

Left Middle: *Operating an overhead powered electric railway, a need exists for an overhead power line maintenance vehicle, enabling staff to reach the overhead equipment and provide a rapid repair. The overhead repair team are based at Laxey (mid way along the line) and have at their disposal rebuilt ex passenger car No. 52 which is now modified as a works vehicle and has a central lift platform. When needed a power car is used to haul the works vehicle to site. No. 52 is seen inside the shed at Laxey.* **CJM**

Locomotive

Number/Name	Type	Builder	Year
LM344 *Pig*	60SL 4-wheel	Simplex	1980

Works No. 60SL751, ex-Bord na Mona Peat Railway, Ireland as No. LM344.

Currently working on Manx Electric Railway from Dhoon.

Right: *Although not owned by the railway, Loco LM344 once named Pig was a previous railway asset now operated by contractor Auldyn. The loco is used at work sites on either the electric or steam railway, usually to operate ballast or rail trains. It has been rebuilt in recent years and now sports train air brakes and a revised front end. It is seen near Dhoon with a ballast train in summer 2018.* **CJM**

Snaefell Mountain Railway

The Snaefell Mountain Railway is a 3ft 6in (1067mm)-gauge twin-track line which operates from Laxey to Snaefell Summit, a distance of 5 miles (8km). It is energised at 550V dc using the overhead power collection system. The line climbs the Snaefell Mountain and reaches 2,034ft (620m) above sea level. The depot is located at Laxey, where there is a passenger interchange with the Manx Electric Railway. Trains operate only between April and September.

Power Cars

Number	Type	Builder	Year
1	Vestibuled saloon	G F Milnes	1895
2	Vestibuled saloon	G F Milnes	1895
4	Vestibuled saloon	G F Milnes	1895
5§	Vestibuled saloon	H D Kinnin	1971
6	Vestibuled saloon	G F Milnes	1895

§ Original Car No. 5 destroyed by fire in August 1970

Above: *One of the highlights of a visit to the Isle of Man Railways is a trip from Laxey to Snaefell, using the Snaefell Mountain Railway. This self contained 3ft 6in (1067mm) gauge line currently operates a fleet of five twin-cabbed enclosed vehicles. Nos. 1, 2, 4 and 6 were built in 1895 by Milnes of Birkenhead. No. 4 restored to green and white livery is seen at Summit.* **CJM**

Right: *Car No. 5, is a modern rebuild, constructed on the Island in 1971 to replace a fire damaged car of the same number. Looking every bit like the older cars, No. 5 is seen in SMR red and teak colours at Laxey.* **CJM**

Freight and Service Vehicles

Number	Type	Builder	Year
-	Flat wagon	MER	1981
-	Flat wagon	P Keefe	?
-	Flat / tipper	Allens	1940
-	Tower wagon	MER	1998
4	Wickham (11730)	Wickham	1991

Douglas Bay Horse Tramway

One of the only remaining commercial horse-drawn tramways in the world, the Douglas Horse Tramway operates during the summer months between Douglas Sea Terminal and Derby Castle. The 1.6-mile (2.6km) 3ft (914mm)-gauge line is twin track and operates between 09.00 and 18.00. The horses are stabled near to Derby Castle and the welfare of the animals is uppermost in the operation, with each horse working only two or three return trips before returning to 'depot'.

Horses (2019-season)

Alec
Amby
Andrew
Bobby
Charles
Chloe
Douglas
Ginger+
Harry
Keith
Kewin
Nelson
Mary+
Philip
Robin
Rocky
Torin
William
Zeba+

+ Training in 2019

The above horses are rostered to operate the 2019 season.

Left Upper: *The 1.6 mile (2.6km) Douglas Bay Horse Tram is one of the main tourist attractions on the Isle of Man. Operating most days of the week during the summer season it runs between Douglas Sea Terminal and Derby Castle. Some redevelopment of the line is planned for 2019-2020 with the line being moved from the middle of the road to the seaside path to reduce road congestion. Powered by* Keith, *car No. 36, a Toastrack saloon built in 1896 is seen heading towards Derby Castle outside the Palace Hotel.* **CJM**

Left Lower: *With* Bobby *posing for the camera at Derby Castle, Car 44, built by United Electric in 1907 and known as the 'Royal Car' pulls away and heads for the Sea Terminal.* **CJM**

Passenger Trailer Cars

Number	Type	Builder	Year
1	Single-ended saloon	Milnes Voss	1913
11(S§)	Toastrack saloon	Starbuck	1886
12	Toastrack saloon	G F Milnes	1888
14±	Double-deck car	Metro C&W	1883
18	Double-deck car	Metro C&W	1883
21	Toastrack saloon	G F Milnes	1890
22 (S§)	Toastrack saloon	G F Milnes	1890
27	Single-deck saloon	G F Milnes	1892
29	Single-deck saloon	G F Milnes	1892
32	Toastrack saloon	G F Milnes	1896
35■	Toastrack saloon	G F Milnes	1896
36	Toastrack saloon	G F Milnes	1896
38	Toastrack saloon	G F Milnes	1902
42	Toastrack saloon	G F Milnes	1905
43	Toastrack saloon	United Elec	1907
44	Toastrack saloon	United Elec	1907*
45	Toastrack saloon	Milnes Voss	1908
47(S§)	Toastrack saloon	Milnes Voss	1911

* Royal Car
S§ Stored / displayed at Jurby Transport Museum
± Preserved by National Railway Museum at Manx Museum, Douglas
■ Located at Home of Rest for Old Horses, Douglas

Above: *Both open and enclosed cars are available on the Douglas Bay Horse Tramway, and during inclement weather the enclosed vehicles are usually rostered. No. 1, an enclosed single ended saloon was built by Milnes in 1913 and has recently been superbly restored at Derby Castle. The vehicle is seen parked at Derby Castle station.* **CJM**

Below: *Horse Tramcar No. 45, built by Milnes in 1908 is a double ended open Toastrack car, offering little or no protection to passengers or staff in poor weather. The ticket seller on the tram makes his way along the outside of the vehicle whilst it is in motion, hoping that the road traffic does not get too close. No. 45 is powered by* Rocky. **CJM**

Isle of Man Steam Railway

The Isle of Man Steam Railway is a 3ft (914mm)-gauge line operating from Douglas to Port Erin, a distance of 15.3 miles (24.6km). The main depot and workshop is located at Douglas and much of the railway is single line with passing places at most stations. The railway usually operates four round trips each day. The line is mainly operated by steam traction, but a diesel is available and sometimes operates the line's popular dining train.

Locomotives

Steam

Number	Name	Builder	Wheel Arrangement	Year built	Notes
1(S)	*Sutherland*	Beyer Peacock	2-4-0T	1873	
4(S)	*Loch*	Beyer Peacock	2-4-0T	1874	
5(S)	*Mona*	Beyer Peacock	2-4-0T	1874	
6	*Peveril*	Beyer Peacock	2-4-0T	1875	In Museum at Port Erin
8	*Fenella*	Beyer Peacock	2-4-0T	1894	
9(S)	*Douglas*	Beyer Peacock	2-4-0T	1896	
10	*G. H. Wood*	Beyer Peacock	2-4-0T	1905	
11(S)	*Maitland*	Beyer Peacock	2-4-0T	1905	
12	*Hutchinson*	Beyer Peacock	2-4-0T	1908	
13	*Kissack*	Beyer Peacock	2-4-0T	1910	
15	*Caledonia*	Dubs & Co	0-6-0T	1885	
16	*Mannin*	Beyer Peacock	2-4-0T	1926	In Museum at Port Erin

Diesel

Number	Name	Builder	Wheel Arrangement	Year built	Notes
17(S)	*Viking*	Schoema	0-4-0	1958	Diesel-hydraulic - out of use
18	*Ailsa*	Hunslet	0-4-0	1994	Diesel pilot loco
21	-	Motive Power	Bo-Bo	2013	MP550-B1 diesel-electric
22	-	D Wickham	4-wheel P	1956	Ex Lochaber Railway
23	-	D Wickham	4-wheel P	1961	Ex Lochaber Railway
24	-	Motorail	4-wheel DM	1959	Ex B & S Massey, Openshaw
25	-	Motorail	4-wheel DM	1966	Ex NCB Kilnhurst

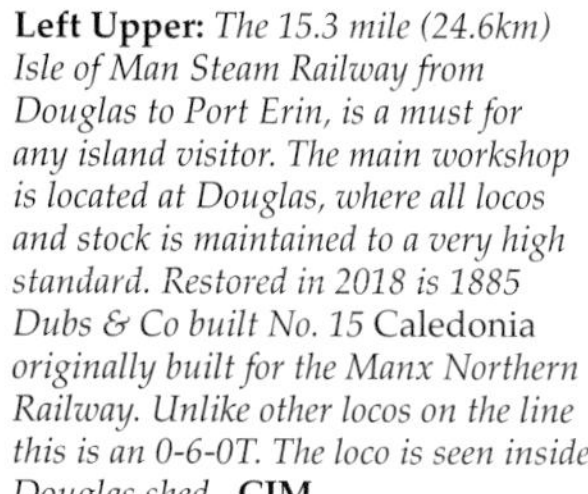

Left Upper: *The 15.3 mile (24.6km) Isle of Man Steam Railway from Douglas to Port Erin, is a must for any island visitor. The main workshop is located at Douglas, where all locos and stock is maintained to a very high standard. Restored in 2018 is 1885 Dubs & Co built No. 15* Caledonia *originally built for the Manx Northern Railway. Unlike other locos on the line this is an 0-6-0T. The loco is seen inside Douglas shed.* **CJM**

Left Lower: *The mainstay of steam power on the IOM Steam Railway is a fleet of Beyer Peacock 2-4-0T locos built in Manchester between 1873 and 1910. No. 8* Fenella *is seen running off shed at Douglas.* **CJM**

Above: *Normally two or three of the lines operational steam locos are in use daily in the running season, depending on which timetable is operating. Under normal running, locos operate with their chimney pointing towards Port Erin. No. 13* Kissack *is seen with a good head of steam with a four coach train approaching Ronaldsway Airport Halt bound for Douglas.* **CJM**

Right Middle: *Loco No. 12* Hutchinson, *painted in Indian red, passes through the countryside at Keristal between Douglas and Port Soderick. Each one of the locos is slightly different with recognition points, for example No. 12 has its number applied above the nameplate, rather than on the chimney.* **CJM**

Right Lower: *The line has one main line diesel loco, No. 21, built by Motive Power Industries and introduced in 2013. Sadly a number of major technical issues befell this loco, mainly involving the bogies which were secondhand. In 2018 the loco was being re-commissioned and should be available for service in 2019, when it is likely to power the dining train service which runs in the evenings. The loco is seen 'on shed' at Douglas.* **CJM**

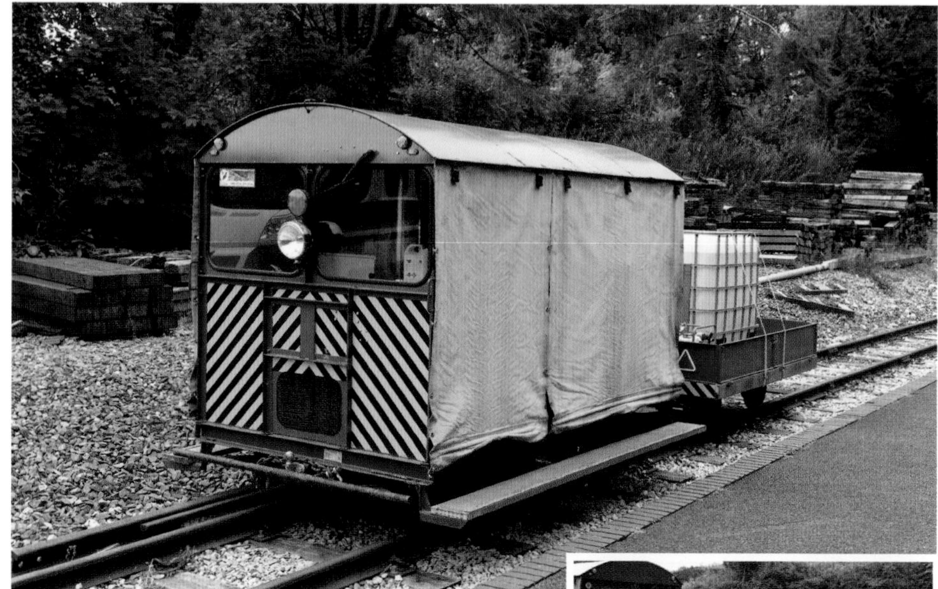

Above and Right: *A number of items of engineering plant operate on the Isle of Man Steam Railway, in the main these are superbly restored to a high standard. Wickham trolley No. 22 a 4-wheel petrol vehicle built in 1956 and previously used on the Lochaber Railway is used for works use and in 2018 was in operation as a fire train out-based at Santon, with a trailer carrying the water supply.* **CJM**

Left: *Simplex/Motorail 4-wheel diesel-mechanical shunting loco No. 25 of 1966, works No. 40S280 is usually kept at Douglas shed and in 2018 carried green livery, with a red buffer beam and Isle of Man Railway badges on both cab sides. The loco is seen inside the shed at Douglas.* **CJM**

Railcars

Number	Builder	Year built	Notes
19(S)	Walker	1949	Ex-County Donegal Railway - out of use
20(S)	Walker	1950	Ex-County Donegal Railway - out of use

Below: *One of the pair of ex County Donegal Railway railcars is seen inside the shed at Douglas in summer 2018 where restoration is continuing, although at a slow pace.* **CJM**

Passenger Coaches

Number	Builder	Style	Year built
F9	Brown Marshalls	Bogie	1881
F10	Brown Marshalls	Bogie	1881
F11	Brown Marshalls	Bogie	1881
F15(S)	Brown Marshalls	Bogie	1894
F18	Brown Marshalls	Bogie	1894
F21(S)	Metropolitan C&W	Bogie	1896
F25(S)	Metropolitan C&W	Bogie	1896
F26	Metropolitan C&W	Bogie	1896
F27	Metropolitan C&W	Bogie	1897 *
F28(S)	Metropolitan C&W	Bogie	1897 *
F29	Metropolitan C&W	Bogie	1905
F30	Metropolitan C&W	Bogie	1905
F31	Metropolitan C&W	Bogie	1905
F32	Metropolitan C&W	Bogie	1905
F35	Metropolitan C&W	Bogie	1905
F36§	Metropolitan C&W	Bogie	1905
F39	Oldbury C & W	Bogie	1887
F43	Metropolitan C&W	Bogie	1908
F45	Metropolitan C&W	Bogie	1913
F46	Metropolitan C&W	Bogie	1913
F47	Metropolitan C&W	Bogie	1923
F48	Metropolitan C&W	Bogie	1923
F49	Metropolitan C&W	Bogie	1926
F54	Metropolitan C&W	Bogie	1923
F63(S)	Metropolitan C&W	Bogie	1920
F66(S)	Metropolitan C&W	Bogie	1920
F67(S)	Metropolitan C&W	Bogie	1920
F74(S)	Metropolitan C&W	Bogie	1921
F75§	Metropolitan C&W	Bogie	1926

* Luggage/Kitchen
§ On display at Port Erin, Museum

Right: *A wonderful collection of preserved original Isle of Man Railway bogie passenger coaches exist, many of which are well in excess of 100 years old. In this view we see car No. F54 a 1923 Metropolitan Railway Carriage and Wagon built saloon. Most passenger stock is finished in red and cream livery.* **CJM**

Left: *Coach No. F49 is one of the 'larger' F series vehicles, built by Metropolitan Carriage & Wagon in 1926, it has three six seat compartments with a luggage and guards van. It was fully restored in 1991-1992 and today is one of the core fleet of passenger carriages. It is seen at Castletown.* **CJM**

Left: *A stunning vehicle is the 'Foxdale Coach', built in 1886 by Oldbury Carriage & Wagon and one of a small number built for the Foxdale branch. It was originally numbered 17 but today also has the identity F39. The coach painted in black and white has four passenger compartments with six seats and a guards van and luggage space. The coach is seen at Port Erin. This vehicle is not usually in daily service.* **CJM**

Left: *Big business for the Isle of Man Railway is the running of dining trains, with one set of coaches specially modified for this purpose, fitted with gangways, central corridors and even a bar car. Food is largely prepared at Douglas and then serviced from a serving vehicle on the train. The service provided is of a very high standard and often trains are fully booked. Car No. F35 originally built in 1905 has been converted to a first class saloon with a bar at the near end, this is equipped to serve draught beer. The vehicle is shown at Douglas.* **CJM**

Left: *Rebuilt with a central gangway with 2+2 side seating, car F32 was originally built in 1905 by Metropolitan Carriage & Wagon as one of the first 37ft 0in long vehicles with a wooden body on a steel underframe. From the 1980s the vehicle has been set aside for the dining train and now sports end gangways. The vehicle is seen at Douglas.* **CJM**

Freight & Service Vehicles

Number	Type	Builder	Year
G1	Van 6-ton	Metropolitan C&W	1873
W2	Well	IOM	1998
WW111	Well	IOM	2014
Gr12	Van 6-ton	Swansea Wagon	1879
G19§	Van 6-ton	IOM	1921
F23	Flat	Metropolitan C&W	1896
F33	Flat	Metropolitan C&W	1905-25
F40	Flat	Metropolitan C&W	1905-25
F41	Flat	Metropolitan C&W	1905-25
F44	Flat	Metropolitan C&W	1905-25
F50	Flat	Metropolitan C&W	1911-25
F57	Flat	Metropolitan C&W	1911-25
F65	Hopper	Metropolitan C&W	1910 *
F70	Hopper	Metropolitan C&W	1922 *
F71	Flat	Metropolitan C&W	1911-25
F73	Flat	Metropolitan C&W	1920
M69(S)	2-plank wagon	Metropolitan C&W	1926
M78	2-plank wagon	Metropolitan C&W	1926
F430	Flat	Hudson	c1980
RF274	Flat	Hudson	c1980

* Coach chassis
§ On display at Port Erin Museum

Right Upper: *A number of freight and service vehicles are on the Isle of Man Steam Railway roster, these are usually kept when not in use at Douglas, with some flat wagons stored at Castletown or Port St Mary. The underframe of former passenger coach F.73 is now a flat wagon and usually used to store sleepers and rail. This vehicle was originally one of the 1920s built 'pairs' coaches* **CJM**

Right Middle: *In 2014 a purpose-built bogie well wagon was built by the railway and given the identity of WW111. It is seen stabled in the siding adjacent to Douglas station.* **CJM**

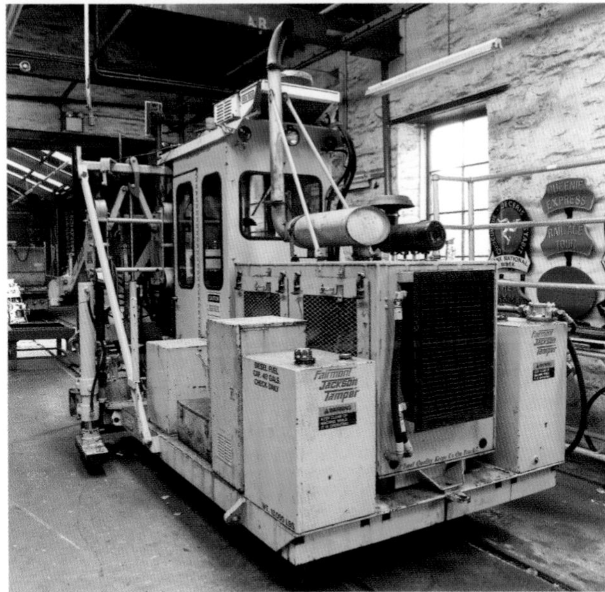

Right Lower: *Track maintenance is very important to the management of the Isle of Man Railway and to assist in keeping the track in good condition, a Fairmont Jackson narrow-gauge tamping machine is on the roster, seen in this illustration inside the shed at Douglas.* **CJM**

UK Heritage Railways

Avon Valley Railway
Bitton Station, Bath Rd, Bristol, South Gloucestershire. BS30 6HD

Battlefield Line
Shackerstone Railway Society Ltd, Shackerstone Station, Shackerstone, Leicestershire. CV13 6NW

Bluebell Railway
The Bluebell Railway, Sheffield Park Station, East Sussex. TN22 3QL

Bodmin & Wenford Railway
Bodmin & Wenford Railway, Bodmin General Station, Bodmin, Cornwall. PL31 1AQ

Bo'ness & Kinneil Railway
Bo'ness & Kinneil Railway, Bo'ness Station, Union St, Bo'ness. EH51 9AQ

Bristol Harbour Railway
Bristol Harbour Railway, Wapping Road, Bristol. BS1 4RN

Buckinghamshire Railway Centre
Quainton Road Station, Station Road, Quainton, Aylesbury. HP22 4BY

Caledonian Railway
Caledonian Railway , The Station, Park Road, Brechin, Angus. DD9 7AF

Chasewater Railway
Chasewater Country Park, Brownhills West Station, Pool Lane, Burntwood, Staffordshire. WS8 7NL

Chinnor & Princes Risborough Railway
Chinnor & Princes Risborough Railway, Station Road, Chinnor, Oxfordshire. OX39 4ER

Cholsey & Wallingford Railway
Cholsey & Wallingford Railway, Wallingford Station, 5 Hithercroft Road, Wallingford, Oxfordshire, OX10 9GQ

Churnet Valley Railway
Churnet Valley Railway, Consall Station, Consall, Leek, Staffordshire, ST13 7EE

Colne Valley Railway
Colne Valley Railway, Castle Hedingham, Halstead. CO9 3DZ

Dartmoor Railway
Dartmoor Railway, Okehampton Railway Station, Station Road, Okehampton. EX20 1EJ

Dean Forest Railway
Dean Forest Railway, Forest Road, Lydney, Gloucestershire. GL15 4ET

Derwent Valley Light Railway
Derwent Valley Light Railway, Murton Park, Murton Lane, Murton, York. YO19 5UF

East Kent Railway
East Kent Railway, Station Road, Shepherdswell, Dover, CT15 7PD

East Lancashire Railway
East Lancashire Railway, Bury Bolton Street Station, Bolton Street, Bury, Lancashire. BL9 0EY

East Somerset Railway
East Somerset Railway, Cranmore Railway Station, Cranmore, Shepton Mallet, Somerset. BA4 4QP

Ecclesbourne Valley Railway
Ecclesbourne Valley Railway, Wirksworth Station, Coldwell Street, Wirksworth, Derbyshire. DE4 4FB

Eden Valley Railway
Eden Valley Railway, Warcop Station, Warcop, Appleby, Cumbria. CA16 6PR

Elsecar Heritage Railway
Elsecar Heritage Railway, The Railway Office, Wath Road, Elsecar, Barnsley, S74 8HJ

Embsay and Bolton Abbey Steam Railway
Embsay Railway, Embsay Station, Embsay, Skipton, North Yorkshire. BD23 6QX

Epping Ongar Railway
Epping Ongar Railway, Ongar Station, Station Approach, Ongar, Essex. CM5 9BN

Foxfield Railway
Foxfield Railway, Foxfield Station, Caverswall Road, Blythe Bridge, Stoke-on-Trent. ST11 9BG

Gloucestershire Warwickshire Railway
Gloucestershire Warwickshire Railway, Railway Station, Toddington, Gloucestershire. GL54 5DT

Great Central Railway
Great Central Railway PLC, Loughborough Central Station, Great Central Road, Loughborough, Leicestershire. LE11 1RW

Great Central Railway (Nottingham)
Great Central Railway - Nottingham, Mere Way, Ruddington, Nottinghamshire. NG11 6JS

Gwili Railway
Gwili Railway, Bronwydd Arms Station, Carmarthen. SA33 6HT

Helston Railway
Helston Railway, Trevarno Farm, Prospidnick, Helston. TR13 0RY

Isle of Wight Steam Railway
Isle of Wight Steam Railway, The Railway Station, Havenstreet, Isle of Wight. PO33 4DS

Kent & East Sussex Steam Railway
Kent & East Sussex Railway, Tenterden Town Station, Station Road, Tenterden, Kent. TN30 6HE

Keith & Dufftown Railway
Keith & Dufftown Railway, Dufftown Station, Dufftown, Banffshire. AB55 4BA

Keighley & Worth Valley Railway
Keighley & Worth Valley Railway, The Railway Station, Haworth, West Yorkshire. BD22 8NJ

Llangollen Railway
Llangollen Railway, The Station, Abbey Road, Llangollen, Denbighshire. LL20 8SN

Llanelli & Mynydd Mawr Railway
Llanelli & Mynydd Mawr Railway, Cynheidre, Llanelli, Carmarthenshire. SA15 5YF

Lavender Line
Lavender Line, Isfield Station, Isfield, Near Uckfield, East Sussex. TN22 5XB

Lakeside & Haverthwaite Railway
Lakeside & Haverthwaite Railway, Haverthwaite Station, Near Ulverston, Cumbria. LA12 8AL

Lincolnshire Wolds Railway
Lincolnshire Wolds Railway, Ludborough Station, Station Road, Ludborough, Lincolnshire, DN36 5SQ

Middleton Railway
Middleton Railway Trust Ltd, The Station, Moor Road, Hunslet, Leeds. LS10 2JQ

Midland Railway Centre
Midland Railway, Butterley Station, Ripley, Derbyshire. DE5 3QZ

Mid Hants Railway
Mid Hants Railway, The Railway Station, Alresford, Hampshire. SO24 9JG

Mid-Norfolk Railway
Mid-Norfolk Railway, Dereham Station, Station Road, Norfolk. NR19 1DF

Mid Suffolk Light Railway
Mid Suffolk Light Railway, Brockford Station, Wetheringsett, Stowmarket, Suffolk. IP14 5PW

Nene Valley Railway
Nene Valley Railway, Wansford Station, Stibbington, Peterborough. PE8 6LR

North Norfolk Railway
North Norfolk Railway, Sheringham Station, Station Approach, Sheringham, Norfolk. NR26 8RA

North Tyneside Steam Railway
Stephenson Railway Museum, Middle Engine Lane, North Shields, Tyne and Wear. NE29 8DX

North Yorkshire Moors Railway
North Yorkshire Moors Railway, Pickering Station, Pickering, North Yorkshire. YO18 7AJ

Northampton & Lamport Railway
Northampton & Lamport Railway, Pitsford & Brampton Station, Pitsford Road, Chapel Brampton, NN6 8BA

Dartmouth Steam Railway
Dartmouth Steam Railway, Queens Park Station, Torbay Road, Paignton, Devon. TQ4 6AF

Peak Rail
Peak Rail, Matlock Station, Matlock, Derbyshire. DE4 3NA

Plym Valley Railway
Plym Valley Railway, Coypool Road, Plympton, Plymouth. PL7 4NW

Pontypool & Blaenavon Railway
Pontypool & Blaenavon Railway, Railway Station, Furnace sidings, Garn Yr Erw, Blaenavon. NP4 9SF

Ribble Steam Railway
Ribble Steam Railway, Chain Caul Road, Preston, Lancashire. PR2 2PD

Royal Deeside Railway
The Royal Deeside Railway, Milton of Crathes, Banchory, Aberdeenshire. AB31 5QH

Severn Valley Railway
Severn Valley Railway, Kidderminster Station, Kidderminster. DY10 1QR

Somerset & Dorset Railway
Somerset & Dorset Railway Heritage Trust, Midsomer Norton Station, Silver Street, Midsomer Norton. BA3 2EY

South Devon Railway
South Devon Railway, Buckfastleigh Station, Dartbridge Road, Buckfastleigh, Devon. TQ11 0DZ

Spa Valley Railway
Spa Valley Railway, Tunbridge Wells West Station, Royal Tunbridge Wells, Kent. TN2 5QY

Strathspey Railway
Strathspey Railway, Aviemore Station, Dalfaber Road, Aviemore, Invernessshire. PH22 1PY

Swanage Railway
Swanage Railway, Station House, Swanage, Dorset. BH19 1HB

Swindon & Cricklade Railway
Swindon & Cricklade Railway, Blunsdon Station, Tadpole Lane, Swindon. SN25 2DA

Tanfield Railway
Tanfield Railway, Marley Hill, Engine Shed, Old Marley Hill, Gateshead. NE16 5ET

Weardale Railway
Weardale Railway, Stanhope Station, County Durham. DL13 2YS

Wensleydale Railway
Wensleydale Railway, Leases Road, Leeming Bar, North Yorkshire. DL7 9AR

West Somerset Railway
West Somerset Railway, The Railway Station, Minehead, Somerset. TA24 5BG

Railway Centres and Museums

Appleby Frodingham Railway
Appleby Frodingham Railway, British Steel, Gate E, Brigg Road, Scunthorpe, Lincolnshire. DN16 1XA

Barrow Hill Roundhouse
Barrow Hill Roundhouse, Campbell Drive, Barrow Hill, Chesterfield, Derbyshire. S43 2PR

Beamish Museum & Railway Centre
Beamish Museum, Beamish, County Durham. DH9 0RG

Bideford Railway Heritage Centre
Bideford Railway Centre, Bideford Station, Bideford, Devon. EX39 4BB

Bressingham Steam & Gardens
Bressingham Steam & Gardens, Low Road, Bressingham, Diss, Norfolk. IP22 2AA

Crewe Heritage Centre (The Railway Age)
The Railway Age, Vernon Way, Crewe. CW1 2DB

Didcot Railway Centre
Didcot Parkway railway station, Didcot, Oxfordshire. OX11 7NJ

East Anglian Railway Museum
East Anglian Railway Museum, Chappel Station, Colchester, Essex. CO6 2DS

Glasgow Museum of Transport (Riverside Museum)
Riverside Museum, Pointhouse Place, Glasgow. G3 8RS

Head of Steam, Darlington
Head of Steam - Darlington Railway Museum, Station Road, Darlington. DL3 6ST

Locomotion, Shildon (National Railway Museum)
Locomotion - National Railway Museum, Dale Road Industrial Estate, Dale Road, Shildon, County Durham. DL4 2RE

London Transport Museum
Covent Garden Piazza, London. WC2E 7BB

London Transport Museum Depot
118-120 Gunnersbury Lane, Acton Town, London. W3 9BQ

Mangapps Railway Museum
Mangapps Railway Museum, Southminster Road, Burnham-on-Crouch, Essex. CM0 8QG

Monkwearmouth Station Museum
Monkwearmouth Station Museum , North Bridge Street, Sunderland. SR5 1AP

National Railway Museum
National Railway Museum, Leeman Road, York. YO26 4XJ

Rocks by Rail (Rutland Railway Museum)
Rocks by Rail, Ashwell Road, Cottesmore, Oakham, Leicestershire, LE15 7FF

Rushden Transport Museum
Rushden Transport Museum, Rushden Station, Station Approach, Rushden, Northamptonshire. NN10 0AW

Stainmore Railway
Stainmore Railway, Station Road, Kirkby Stephen, Cumbria. CA17 4LA

Steam – Museum of the Great Western Railway
Steam, Fire Fly Avenue, Swindon. SN2 2EY

Telford Steam Railway
Telford Steam Railway, The Old Loco Shed, Bridge Road, Horsehay, Telford, Shropshire. TF4 3UH

Tyseley Railway Centre
Vintage Trains, 670 Warwick Road, Tyseley, Birmingham. B11 2HL

Vale of Berkeley Railway Museum
Vale of Berkeley Railway, The Old Engine House, Dock Road, Sharpness, Gloucestershire. GL13 9UD

Yeovil Railway Centre
Yeovil Railway Centre, Yeovil Junction Station, Stoford, Yeovil, Somerset. BA22 9UU

Above: *A1X 0-6-0T No. W11 Newport is seen working on the Isle of Wight Steam Railway at Havenstreet. In BR days, this was numbered 32640.* **CJM**

Heritage Railways

Above: *It is not uncommon for preserved steam locomotives to take on different identities, to either mark special events or operate photographic charters. Here, Swanage-based Class 4 2-6-4T No. 80104 is seen working as sister loco No. 80146. The loco and Mk1 formation is seen arriving at Corfe Castle.* **CJM**

Below: *Great Western Railway 1920s built 4575 class 'Small Prairie' No. 5541, is preserved at the Dean Forest Railway and is recorded passing Norchard with a Parkend to Lydney train.* **Antony Christie**

Heritage Railways

Above: *1930-built Great Western Railway 'King' No. 6023* King Edward II *is a true marvel of preservation, being purchased in scrap condition from Barry and restored at Didcot to fully operational condition. Carrying BR blue livery, the loco has visited a number of railways. It was proposed to put the loco onto the main line, but these plans have now been sidelined. In summer 2018 the loco was operated on the Paignton & Dartmouth Railway, seen here crossing Broadsands Viaduct.* **Antony Christie**

Below: *Today, preservation of main line diesel locomotives is big business, with several members of the more popular classes fully restored and operating on preserved railways throughout the country. Class 37/0 No. 37142 has been fully restored by a dedicated team at the Bodmin and Wenford Railway in Cornwall, where the loco is seen in summer 2018.* **Antony Christie**

Above: *The picturesque South Devon Railway, running adjacent to the River Dart, offers some amazing photographic viewpoints. Here SDR-based 0-6-0 Pannier No. 6412 with a Great Western auto coach is seen near Hood Bridge.* **Antony Christie**

Below: *In addition to operating former main line locomotives a number of preserved railways work a fleet of former industrial locomotives. On the Bo'ness and Kinneil Railway in Scotland 0-6-0ST 'Austerity' No. 19, built in 1954 and saved from Comrie Colliery can be found.* **Antony Christie**

Above: *The National Railway Museum, in addition to having their main base at York, operate a satellite site at Shildon, a rail connected site, where a number of exhibits can be found, including a number of 'modern traction' items.* **Antony Christie**

Below: *The restoration standards of modern traction, diesel and electric locos in the UK, is to a very high standard, and a diverse selection of liveries have been applied allowing todays enthusiasts the chance to see colours of the past. Showing the BR 'Dutch' livery, Class 31 No. 31206 is seen at Wirksworth on the Ecclesbourne Valley Railway.* **Antony Christie**

Preserved Modern Traction - Locomotives

Class 01

D2953	(11503)	Peak Rail, Heritage Shunters Trust
D2956	(11506)	East Lancashire Railway

Class 02

(D2853)	02003	Barrow Hill Roundhouse
D2854		Peak Rail, Heritage Shunters Trust
D2858		Midland Railway Centre
D2860		National Railway Museum
D2866		Peak Rail, Heritage Shunters Trust
D2867		Battlefield Railway
D2868		Barrow Hill

Class 03

(03018)	(D2018)	Mangapps Farm - as 11205
(03020)	(D2020)	Sonic Rail Services, Burnham - 11207
(03022)	(D2022)	Swindon & Cricklade Railway - 11209
(D2023)		Kent & East Sussex Railway - 11210
(D2024)		Kent & East Sussex Railway - 11211
03027	D2027	Peak Rail, Heritage Shunters Trust
03037	D2037	Royal Deeside Railway
D2041		Colne Valley Railway
D2046		Plym Valley Railway
D2051		North Norfolk Railway
03059	D2059	Isle of Wight Steam Railway
03062	D2062	East Lancashire Railway
03063	D2063	North Norfolk Railway
03066	D2066	Barrow Hill Roundhouse
03069	D2069	Vale of Berkeley Railway
03072	D2072	Lakeside & Haverthwaite Railway
03073	D2073	Railway Age, Crewe
03078	D2078	North Tyneside Steam Railway
03079	D2079	Derwent Valley Light Railway
03081	D2081	Mangapps Farm Railway Museum
03084	D2084	East Lancashire Railway
03089	D2089	Mangapps Farm Railway Museum
03090	D2090	National Railway Museum - Shildon
03094	D2094	Royal Deeside Railway
03099	D2099	Peak Rail, Heritage Shunters Trust
03112	D2112	Rother Valley Railway
03113	D2113	Peak Rail, Heritage Shunters Trust
D2117		Lakeside & Haverthwaite Rly - No. 8
D2118		Great Central Railway, Nottingham
03119	D2119	Epping & Ongar Railway
03120	D2120	Fawley Hill Railway
03128	D2128	Peak Rail, Rowsley
D2133		West Somerset Railway
03134	D2134	Royal Deeside Railway
D2138		Midland Railway Centre, Butterley
D2139		Peak Rail, Heritage Shunters Trust
03141	D2141	Pontypool & Blaenavon Railway
03144	D2144	Wensleydale Railway
03145	D2145	Moreton Park Rly, Moreton-on-Lugg
D2148		Ribble Steam Railway
03152	D2152	Swindon & Cricklade Railway
03158	D2158	Titley Junction, Herefordshire
03162	D2162	Llangollen Railway
03170	D2170	Epping and Ongar Railway
D2178		Gwili Railway
03179	D2179	Rushden Transport Museum
03180	D2180	Peak Rail, Rowsley
D2182		Gloucester Warwickshire Railway
D2184		Colne Valley Railway
03189	D2189	Ribble Steam Railway
D2192		Dartmouth Steam Railway
D2196		WCRC Carnforth
03197	D2197	Mid Norfolk Railway
D2199		Peak Rail, Heritage Shunters Trust
03371	D2371	Dartmouth Steam Railway
03399	D2399	Mangapps Farm Railway

Class 04

D2203	11103	Embsay & Bolton Abbey Railway
D2205		Peak Rail, Heritage Shunters Trust
D2207	11108	North Yorkshire Moors Railway
D2229	11135	Peak Rail, Heritage Shunters Trust
D2245	11215	Derwent Valley Light Railway
D2246		South Devon Railway
D2271		South Devon Railway
D2272		Peak Rail, Heritage Shunters Trust
D2279		East Anglian Railway
D2280		North Norfolk Railway
D2284		Peak Rail, Heritage Shunters Trust
D2289		Peak Rail, Heritage Shunters Trust
D2298		Buckinghamshire Railway Centre
D2302		Moreton Park Rly - Moreton-on-Lugg
D2310		Battlefield Railway, Shackerstone
D2324		Peak Rail, Heritage Shunters Trust
D2325		Mangapps Farm Railway
D2334		Mid Norfolk Railway
D2337		Peak Rail, Heritage Shunters Trust

Class 05

05001	D2554	Isle of Wight Steam Railway
D2578		Moreton Park Rly - Moreton-on-Lugg
D2587		Peak Rail, Heritage Shunters Trust
D2595		Ribble Steam Railway

Class 06

06003	D2420	Peak Rail, Heritage Shunters Trust

Class 07

07001	D2985	Peak Rail, Heritage Shunters Trust
07005	D2989	Great Central Railway
07010	D2994	Avon Valley Railway
07011	D2995	St. Leonards Railway Engineering
07012	D2996	Barrow Hill Roundhouse
07013	D2997	East Lancashire Railway

Classes 08, 09 and 10

D3000		Peak Rail
D3002	13002	Plym Valley Railway
D3014		Dartmouth Steam Railway
08011	D3018	Chinnor & Princes Risborough Rly
08012	D3019	Cambrian Heritage Railways
08015	D3022	Severn Valley Railway - as 13022
08016	D3023	Peak Rail, HST - as 13023
08021	D3029	Tyseley Locomotive Works - as 13029
08022	D3030	Cholsey & Wallingford Rly - as 13030
08032	D3044	Mid Hants Railway - as 13044
08046	D3059	Caledonian Rly, Brechin - as 13059
08054	D3067	Embsay & Bolton Abbey Railway
08060	D3074	Cholsey & Wallingford Rly - as 13074
08064	D3079	National Railway Museum - as 13079
D3101	13101	Great Central Rly, Loughborough
08102	D3167	Lincolnshire Wolds Railway
08108	D3174	Kent & East Sussex Railway - as 13174
08114	D3180	Great Central Rly, Nottingham

08123	D3190	Cholsey & Wallingford Railway
08133	D3201	Severn Valley Railway - as 13201
08164	D3232	East Lancashire Railway - as 13232
08168	D3236	Nemesis Rail - Burton-on-Trent
D3261		Swindon & Cricklade Rly - as 13261
08195	D3265	Llangollen Railway - as 13265
08202	D3272	Avon Valley Railway
08220	D3290	GCR, Nottingham - at EMD Longport
08238	D3308	Dean Forest Railway - as 13308
08266	D3336	Keighley & Worth Valley Railway
08288	D3358	Mid Hants Railway
08331	D3401	Midland Railway Centre - Butterley
08359	D3429	Telford Steam Railway
08377	D3462	Mid Hants Railway
08436	D3551	Swanage Railway
08443	D3558	Bo'ness & Kinneil Railway
08444	D3559	Bodmin & Wenford Railway
08471	D3586	Severn Valley Railway
08473	D3588	Dean Forest Railway (parts only)
08476	D3591	Swanage Railway
08479	D3594	East Lancashire Railway
08490	D3605	Strathspey Railway
08495	D3610	North Yorkshire Moors Railway
08503	D3658	Vale of Glamorgan Railway
08507	D3662	LNWR, Crewe
08528	D3690	Great Central Railway, Loughborough
08556	D3723	North Yorkshire Moors Railway
08590	D3757	Midland Railway Centre
08604	D3771	Didcot Railway Centre
08605	D3772	Ecclesbourne Valley Railway
08631	D3798	LNWR, Crewe
08633	D3800	Churnet Valley Railway
08635	D3802	Severn Valley Railway
08685	D3852	East Kent Railway
08694	D3861	Great Central Railway, Loughborough
08700	D3867	HNRC at Bombardier Ilford
08704	D3871	Ecclesbourne Valley Railway
08737	D3905	LNWR, Crewe
08742	D3910	East Kent Light Railway
08757	D3925	Telford Steam Railway
08767	D3935	North Norfolk Railway
08769	D3937	Dean Forest Railway
08772	D3940	North Norfolk Railway
08773	D3941	Embsay & Bolton Abbey Railway
08780	D3948	WCR Southall
08784	D3952	Great Central Railway, Nottingham
08825	D3993	Chinnor & Princes Risborough Rly
08830	D3998	Peak Rail, Rowsley
08850	D4018	North Yorkshire Moors Railway
08881	D4095	Somerset & Dorset Railway
08888	D4118	Kent & East Sussex Railway Stored
08896	D4126	Severn Valley Railway
08907	D4137	Great Central Railway, Loughborough
08911	D4141	National Railway Museum
08915	D4145	North Tyneside Steam Railway
08922	D4152	Great Central Railway, Nottingham
08937	D4167	Dartmoor Railway
08944	D4174	East Lancashire Railway
08993	D3759	Keighley & Worth Valley Railway
09001	D3665	Peak Rail, Rowsley
09004	D3668	Swindon & Cricklade Railway
09010	D3721	South Devon Railway
09012	D4100	Severn Valley Railway
09015	D4103	Rye Farm, Wishaw
09017	D4105	National Railway Museum
09018	D4106	Bluebell Railway
09019	D4107	West Somerset Railway
09024	D4112	East Lancashire Railway
09025	D4113	Lavender Line
09026	D4114	Spa Valley Railway
09107	D4013	Severn Valley Railway
D3452		Bodmin & Wenford Railway
D3489		Spa Valley Railway
D4067		Great Central Rly, Loughborough
D4092		Barrow Hill Roundhouse

Class 11

12052	Caledonian Railway
12077	Midland Railway Centre - Butterley
12082	Mid Hants Railway
12083	Battlefield Railway
12088	Aln Valley Railway
12093	Caledonian Railway
12099	Severn Valley Railway
12131	North Norfolk Railway
12139	North Yorkshire Moors Railway

Class 12

15224	Spa Valley Line

Class 14

D9500	Peak Rail, Rowsley
D9502	East Lancs Railway
D9504	Kent and East Sussex Railway
D9513	Embsay and Bolton Abbey Railway
D9516	Didcot Railway Centre
D9518	West Somerset Railway
D9520	Nene Valley Railway
D9521	Dean Forest Railway
D9523	Nene Valley Railway
D9524	Churnet Valley Railway
D9525	Peak Rail, Heritage Shunters Trust
D9526	West Somerset Railway
D9529	Nene Valley Railway
D9531	East Lancs Railway
D9537	Ecclesbourne Valley Railway
D9539	Ribble Steam Railway
D9551	Severn Valley Railway
D9553	Vale of Berkeley Railway
D9555	Dean Forest Railway

Class 15

D8233	East Lancs Railway

Class 17

D8568	Chinnor & Princes Risborough Rly

Class 20

20050	D8000	National Railway Museum
20001	D8001	Ecclesbourne Valley Railway
20007§	D8007	Nottingham Transport Centre
20020	D8020	Bo'ness & Kinneil Railway SRPS
20031	D8031	Keighley & Worth Valley Railway
20035	D8035	Gloucester Warwickshire Railway
20048	D8048	Midland Railway Centre
20057	D8057	Churnet Valley Railway
20059	D8059	Midland Railway Centre
20063	D8063	Battlefield Railway, Shackerstone
20069	D8069	Mid Norfolk Railway
20087	D8087	East Lancashire Railway
20098	D8098	Nottingham Transport Centre
20105	D8105	Barrow Hill Roundhouse

20110	D8110	East Lancashire Railway HNRC
20228	D8128	Barry Rail Centre
20137	D8137	Gloucester Warwickshire Railway
20154	D8154	Great Central Railway, Nottingham
20166	D8166	Wensleydale Railway HNRC
20177	D8177	Severn Valley Railway
20188	D8188	Midland Railway Centre
20205	D8305	Midland Railway Centre
20214	D8314	Lakeside & Haverthwaite Railway
20227	D8327	North Norfolk Railway

Class 24

24032	D5032	North Yorkshire Moors Railway
24054	D5054	East Lancashire Railway
24061	D5061	North Yorkshire Moors Railway
24081	D5081	Gloucestershire Warwickshire Rly

Class 25

25035	D5185	Great Central Railway
25057	D5207	North Norfolk Railway (HNRC)
25059	D5209	Keighley & Worth Valley Railway
25067	D5217	Nemesis Rail, Burton-on-Trent
25072	D5222	Caledonian Railway, Brechin
25083	D5233	Caledonian Railway, Brechin
25173	D7523	Battlefield Line, Shackerstone
25185	D7535	South Devon Railway
25191	D7541	South Devon Railway
25235	D7585	Bo'ness & Kinneil Railway
25244	D7594	Kent & East Sussex Railway
25901	D7612	South Devon Railway
25265	D7615	Nemesis Rail - Burton-on-Trent
25278	D7628	North Yorkshire Moors Railway
25279	D7629	Great Central Railway, Nottingham
25904	D7633	HNRC
25309	D7659	Peak Rail
25313	D7663	Wensleydale Railway (HNRC)
25321	D7671	Midland Railway Centre
25912	D7672	Churnet Valley Railway

Class 26 and 27

26007	D5300	Barrow Hill Roundhouse
26001	D5301	Caledonian Railway
26002	D5302	Strathspey Railway
26004	D5304	Nemesis Rail - Burton-on-Trent
26010	D5310	Llangollen Railway
26011	D5311	Nemesis Rail - Burton-on-Trent
26014	D5314	Caledonian Railway, Brechin
26024	D5324	Bo'ness & Kinneil Railway
26025	D5325	Strathspey Railway
26035	D5335	Caledonian Railway, Brechin
26038	D5338	North Yorkshire Moors Railway
26040	D5340	Whitrope Heritage Centre
26043	D5343	Gloucestershire Warwickshire Rly
27001	D5347	Bo'ness & Kinneil Railway
27005	D5351	Bo'ness & Kinneil Railway
27007	D5353	Goodman's Yard - Wishaw
27024	D5370	Caledonian Railway, Brechin
27066	D5386	Barrow Hill Roundhouse
27050	D5394	Strathspey Railway
27056	D5401	Great Central Railway
27059	D5410	UKRL Leicester

Class 28

D5705		East Lancashire Railway

Class 31

31018	D5500	National Railway Museum
31101	D5518	Avon Valley Railway
31105	D5523	Mangapps Farm
31418	D5522	Midland Railway Centre
31108	D5526	Midland Railway Centre
31466	D5533	Dean Forest Railway
31119	D5537	Embsay & Bolton Abbey Railway
31128	D5546	Nemesis Rail - Burton-on-Trent
31461	D5547	Nemesis Rail - Burton-on-Trent
31130	D5548	Avon Valley Railway
31438	D5557	Epping and Ongar Railway
31162	D5580	Great Central Railway, Nottingham
31163	D5581	Chinnor & Princes Ris Rly (as 97205)
31435	D5600	Embsay & Bolton Abbey Railway
31190	D5613	Weardale Railway
31203	D5627	Pontypool & Blaenavon Railway
31206	D5630	Ecclesbourne Valley Railway
31207	D5631	North Norfolk Railway
31210	D5634	Dean Forest Railway
31233	D5660	Mangapps Farm
31235	D5662	Dean Forest Railway
31255	D5683	Mid Norfolk Railway
31430	D5695	Spa Valley Railway
31270	D5800	Peak Rail, Rowsley
31271	D5801	Nene Valley Railway
31452	D5809	Weardale Railway
31414	D5814	Midland Railway Centre
31289	D5821	Northampton & Lamport Railway
31297	D5830	Great Central Rly, Loughborough
31327	D5862	Strathspey Railway
31601	D5609	Ecclesbourne Valley Railway

Class 33

33002	D6501	South Devon Railway
33008	D6508	Battlefield Railway
33102	D6513	Churnet Valley Railway
33103	D6514	Ecclesbourne Valley Railway
33012	D6515	Swanage Railway
33108	D6521	Severn Valley Railway
33109	D6525	East Lancashire Railway
33110	D6527	Bodmin & Wenford Railway
33111	D6528	Swanage Railway
33018	D6530	Midland Railway, Butterley
33115	D6533	St. Leonards Railway Engineering
33019	D6534	Battlefield Railway
33116	D6535	Great Central Railway, Nottingham
33117	D6536	East Lancashire Railway
33021	D6539	Churnet Valley Railway
33035	D6553	Wensleydale Railway
33046	D6564	East Lancashire Railway
33048	D6566	West Somerset Railway
33052	D6570	Kent & East Sussex Railway
33053	D6571	Leicester
33057	D6575	West Somerset Railway
33063	D6583	Spa Valley Railway
33065	D6585	Spa Valley Railway
33201	D6586	Swanage Railway
33202	D6587	Mid Norfolk Railway
33208	D6593	Battlefield Railway

Class 35

D7017		West Somerset Railway
D7018		West Somerset Railway
D7029		Severn Valley Railway
D7076		East Lancashire Railway

Class 37

37308	D6608	Dean Forest Railway
37119	D6700	National Railway Museum
37003	D6703	Mid Norfolk Railway

37009	D6709	Great Central Railway, Nottingham
37023	D6723	Allely's Yard, Studley
37714	D6724	Great Central Rly, Loughborough
37029	D6729	Epping and Ongar Railway
37032	D6732	Barrow Hill
37037	D6737	South Devon Railway
37042	D6742	Eden Valley Railway, Warcop
37075	D6775	Keighley & Worth Valley Railway
37097	D6797	Caledonian Railway, Brechin
37108	D6808	Crewe Heritage Centre
37109	D6809	East Lancashire Railway
37521	D6817	Barrow Hill Roundhouse
37679	D6823	East Lancashire Railway
37142	D6842	Bodmin & Wenford Railway
37146	D6846	Wensleydale Railway
37901	D6850	Mid Hants Railway
37152	D6852	Peak Rail, Rowsley
37159	D6859	Barrow Hill Roundhouse
37674	D6869	Wensleydale Railway
37188	D6888	Barrow Hill
37190	D6890	Midland Railway Centre
37688	D6905	Severn Valley Railway
37215	D6915	Gloucester & Warwickshire Railway
37216	D6916	Pontypool & Blaenavon Railway
37227	D6927	Chinnor & Princes Risborough Rly
37240	D6940	Bowden Rail, Nottinghm for main line
37248	D6948	Gloucester & Warwickshire Railway
37250	D6950	Wensleydale Railway
37255	D6955	Nemesis Rail, Burton-on-Trent
37261	D6961	Bo'ness & Kinneil Railway
37263	D6963	Telford Steam Railway
37264	D6964	North Yorkshire Moors Railway
37418	D6971	Barrow Hill Roundhouse
37275	D6975	Paignton & Dartmouth Railway
37294	D6994	Embsay & Bolton Abbey Railway

Class 40

40122	D200	National Railway Museum
40012	D212	Barrow Hill Roundhouse
40013§	D213	Loco Services Crewe
40106	D306	East Lancashire Railway
40118	D318	Tyseley Locomotive Works
40135	D335	East Lancashire Railway
40145§	D345	East Lancashire Railway

Class 41

43000	41001	National Railway Museum at Ruddington

Class 42

D821		Severn Valley Railway
D832		East Lancashire Railway

Class 44

44004	D4	Midland Railway Centre - Butterley
44008	D8	Peak Rail, Rowsley

Class 45

45015	D14	Battlefield, Railway
45060	D100	Barrow Hill Roundhouse
45108	D120	East Lancashire Railway
45125	D123	Great Central Rly, Loughborough
45149	D135	Gloucester & Warwickshire Railway
45132	D22	Epping & Ongar Railway
45133	D40	Midland Railway Centre -Butterley
45041	D53	Nene Valley Railway
45112	D61	Nemesis Rail, Burton-on-Trent
45105	D86	Barrow Hill Roundhouse
45135	D99	East Lancashire Railway

Class 46

46010	D147	Great Central Railway, Nottingham
46035	D172	Crewe Heritage Centre
46045	D182	Midland Railway Centre

Class 47

47524	D1107	Churnet Valley Railway
47401	D1500	Midland Railway Centre
47402	D1501	East Lancashire Railway
47417	D1516	Midland Railway Centre
47004	D1524	Embsay & Bolton Abbey Railway
47449	D1566	Llangollen Railway
47635	D1606	Epping & Ongar Railway
47761	D1619	Midland Railway Centre
47765	D1643	East Lancashire Railway
47799	D1654	Eden Valley Railway
47798	D1656	National Railway Museum
47840	D1661	West Somerset Railway
47484	D1662	Rye Farm - Wishaw (Pioneer DG)
47105	D1693	Gloucester Warwickshire Railway
47117	D1705	Great Central Rly, Loughborough
47488	D1713	Nemesis Rail, Burton-on-Trent
47773	D1755	Tyseley Locomotive Works
47580	D1762	Stratford 47 Group
47579	D1778	Mid Hants Railway
47306	D1787	Bodmin Steam Railway
47192	D1842	Weardale Railway
47205	D1855	Northampton & Lamport Railway
47367	D1886	Mid Norfolk Railway
47376	D1895	Gloucester Warwickshire Railway
47785	D1909	Stainmore Railway
47640	D1921	Battlefield Railway, Shackerstone
47744	D1927	Nemesis Rail - Burton-on-Trent
47701	D1932	Nemesis Rail - Burton-on-Trent
47596	D1933	Mid-Norfolk Railway
47712	D1948	Crewe Heritage Centre (For main line)
47503	D1946	Colne Valley Railway
47714	D1955	Great Central R1y, Loughborough
47643	D1970	Bo'ness & Kinneil Railway
47292	D1994	Great Central Railway, Nottingham
47828	D1966	Dartmoor Railway

Class 50

50002	D402	South Devon Railway
50007§	D407	Boden Engineering, Eastcroft
50008	D408	Boden Engineering, Eastcroft
50015	D415	East Lancashire Railway
50017	D417	Private on Great Central Railway
50019	D419	Mid Norfolk Railway
50021	D421	Arlington Fleet Services - Eastleigh
50026	D426	Arlington Fleet Services - Eastleigh
50027	D427	Mid Hants Railway
50029	D429	Peak Rail - Rowsley
50030	D430	Peak Rail - Rowsley
50031	D431	Severn Valley Railway
50033	D433	Vintage Trains, Severn Valley Railway
50035	D435	Severn Valley Railway
50042	D442	Bodmin & Wenford Railway
50044	D444	Severn Valley Railway
50049§	D449	Severn Valley Railway
50050	D400	Boden Engineering, Eastcroft

Class 52

D1010		West Somerset Railway
D1013		Severn Valley Railway

D1015§		Severn Valley Railway
D1023		National Railway Museum
D1041		East Lancashire Railway
D1048		Midland Railway Centre - Butterley
D1062		Severn Valley Railway

Class 55

55002	D9002	National Railway Museum
55009§	D9009	East Lancashire Railway
55015	D9015	Barrow Hill Roundhouse
55016	D9016	Loco Services, Crewe
55019§	D9019	Barrow Hill Roundhouse
55022§	D9000	Loco Services, Crewe

Class 56

56003		Nene Valley Railway
56006		East Lancashire Railway
56009		EMD Longport
56097		Great Central Railway, Nottingham

Class 58

58012		Battlefield Line
58016		UK Rail Leasing, Leicester
58022		Peak Rail
58023		Battlefield Line
58048		Battlefield Line

Class 71

71001	E5001	Barrow Hill Roundhouse

Class 73

73001	E6001	Dean Forest Railway
73002	E6002	Dean Forest Railway
73003	E6003	Swindon and Cricklade Railway
73110	E6016	Great Central Railway, Nottingham
73114	E6020	Battlefield Railway, Shackerstone
73118	E6024	Barry Railway
73129	E6036	Gloucester Warwickshire Railway
73130	E6037	Barry Railway
73140	E6047	Spa Valley Railway
73210	E6022	Ecclesbourne Valley Railway

Class 76

76020	26020	National Railway Museum

Class 77

E27000		Midland Railway Centre
E27001		Museum of Science & Industry, Manchester
E27003		Workgroup 1501 Rotterdam

Class 81

81002	E3003	Barrow Hill Roundhouse

Class 82

82008	E3054	Barrow Hill Roundhouse

Class 83

83012	E3035	Barrow Hill Roundhouse

Class 84

84001	E3036	National Railway Museum, at Barrow Hill Roundhouse

Class 85

85101	E3061	Barrow Hill Roundhouse

Class 86

86259§	E3137	Willesden Depot
86101§	E3191	Willesden Depot
86401§	E3199	Willesden Depot

Class 87

87001		National Railway Museum
87002§		Willesden Depot
87035		Crewe Heritage Centre

Class 89

89001		Barrow Hill Roundhouse

Class 97

97650	PWM650	Lincolnshire Wolds Railway
97651	PWM651	Swindon & Cricklade Railway
97654	PWM654	Peak Rail, Heritage Shunter Trust

Unclassified locos

18000		Didcot Railway Centre
D0226		Keighley & Worth Valley Railway
D2511		Keighley & Worth Valley Railway
D2767		Bo'ness & Kinneil Railway
D2774		Strathspey Railway
D2959		Telford Steam Railway
D2971		Telford Steam Railway
Deltic	DP1	National Railway Museum

§ Certified for main line operation

Preserved Modern Traction - Diesel Multiple Unit Stock

APT-E National Railway Museum
LEV1 National Railway Museum at Weardale Rly
LEV2 Connecticut Trolley Museum, USA
LEV3 Downpatrick & County Down Railway
RB002 Riverstone Old Corn Railway, USA
RB004 Waverley Route Heritage Centre
GWR 4 National Railway Museum
GWR 20 Kent & East Sussex Railway
GWR 22 Didcot Railway Centre

50015 Midland Railway Centre
50019 Midland Railway Centre
50160 North Yorkshire Moors Railway
50164 North Yorkshire Moors Railway
50170 Ecclesbourne Valley Railway
50193 Great Central Railway
50203 Great Central Railway
50204 North Yorkshire Moors Railway
50222 Barry Island Railway
50253 Ecclesbourne Valley Railway
50256 Wensleydale Railway
50266 Great Centrtal Railway
50321 Great Central Railway
50338 Barry Island Railway
50413 Helston Railway
50416 Llangollen Railway
50437 Llangollen Railway
50447 Llangollen Railway
50454 Llangollen Railway
50455 East Lancashire Railway
50479 Telford Steam Railway
50494 East Lancashire Railway
50517 East Lancashire Railway
50528 Llangollen Railway
50531 Telford Steam Railway
50556 East Lancashire Railway /
50599 Ecclesbourne Valley Railway
50619 Dean Forest Railway
50628 Keith & Dufftown Railway
50632 Pontypool & Blaenavon Railway
50645 Great Central Railway North
50746 Wensleydale Railway
50926 Great Central Railway North
50928 Keighley & Worth Valley Railway
50933 Severn Valley Railway
50971 Kent & East Sussex Railway
50980 Weardale Railway
51017 Bo'ness & Kinneil Railway
51043 Bo'ness & Kinneil Railway
51073 Ecclesbourne Valley Railway
51074 Swindon & Cricklade Railway
51104 Swindon & Cricklade Railway
51118 Midland Railway Centre
51131 Battlefield Line
51138 Great Central Railway North
51151 Great Central Railway North
51187 Cambrian Railway
51188 Ecclesbourne Valley Railway
51189 Keighley & Worth Valley Railway
51192 National Railway Museum at NNR
51205 Cambrian Railway
51210 Wensleydale Railway
51213 East Anglian Railway Museum
51226 Mid Norfolk Railway
51228 Mid Norfolk Railway
51321 Battlefield Line
51339 East Lancashire Railway
51342 Epping & Ongar Railway
51346 Swanage Railway
51347 Gwili Railway
51351 Pontypool & Blaenavon Railway
51352 Long Marston
51353 Wensleydale Railway
51354 Peak Rail
51356 Swanage Railway
51360 Gloucestershire Warwickshire Railway
51363 Gloucestershire Warwickshire Railway
51365 Plym Valley Railway
51367 Strathspey Railway
51370 Whitwell & Reepham Railway
51371 North Somerset Rly at Eastleigh
51372 Gloucestershire Warwickshire Railway
51375 Chinnor and Princes Risborough Rly
51376 Long Marston
51381 Mangapps Farm Museum
51382 East Lancashire Railway
51384 Epping and Ongar Railway
51388 Swanage Railway
51392 Swanage Railway
51396 Peak Rail
51397 Pontypool & Blaenavon Railway
51400 Wensleydale Railway
51401 Gwili Railway
51402 Strathspey Railway
51405 Gloucestershire Warwickshire Railway
51407 Plym Valley Railway
51412 Whitwell & Reepham Stn, Suffolk
51413 North Somerset Rly at Eastleigh
51427 Great Central Railway
51434 Mid Norfolk Railway
51485 East Lancashire Railway
51499 Mid Norfolk Railway
51503 Mid Norfolk Railway
51505 Ecclesbourne Valley Railway
51511 North Yokshire Moors Railway
51512 Cambrian Railway
51562 National Railway Museum
51565 Keighley & Worth Valley Railway
51566 Dean Forest Railway
51567 Ecclesbourne Valley Railway
51568 Keith & Dufftown Railway
51571 Kent & East Sussex Railway
51572 Wensleydale Railway
51591 Midland Railway Centre
51610 Midland Railway Centre
51616 Great Central Railway
51618 Llangollen Railway
51622 Great Central Railway
51625 Midland Railway Centre
51655 Rosyth Dockyard
51663 West Somerset Railway (frame only)
51669 Spa Valley Railway (for sale)
51803 Keighley & Worth Valley Railway
51813 East Lancashire Railway
51842 East Lancashire Railway
51849 Spa Valley Railway (for sale)
51859 West Somerset Railway
51880 West Somerset Railway
51886 Birmingham Railway Museum
51887 West Somerset Railway

51899	Buckingham Railway Centre
51907	Llangollen Railway
51909	East Somerset Railway
51914	Dean Forest Railway
51919	Garw Valley Railway
51922	National Railway Museum
51933	Swanage Railway
51937	Midland Railway Centre
51941	Severn Valley Railway
51942	Mid Norfolk Railway
51947	Bodmin & Wenford Railway
51950	Telford Steam Railway
51990	Strathspey Railway
51993	Tanat Valley Railway
52005	Tanat Valley Railway
52006	Avon Valley Railway
52008	Strathspey Railway
52012	Tanat Valley Railway
52025	Avon Valley Railway
52029	Gloucestershire Warwickshire Railway
52030	Strathspey Railway
52031	Tanat Valley Railway
52044	Pontypool & Blaenavon Railway
52048	Garw Valley Railway
52053	Keith & Dufftown Railway
52054	Weardale Railway
52062	Telford Steam Railway
52064	Severn Valley Railway
52071	Lakeside & Haverthwaite Railway
52077	Lakeside & Haverthwaite Railway
54223	Llangollen Railway
54270	Mid Norfolk Railway
54279	Lavendar Line
54504	Swanage Railway
55000	South Devon Railway
55000	140001 Keith & Dufftown
55001	East Lancashire Railway
55001	140001 Keith & Dufftown
55003	Gloucestershire Warwickshire Railway
55005	Battlefield Line
55006	Ecclesbourne Valley Railway
55009	Mid Norfolk Railway
55012	Weardale Railway
55019	Llanelli & Mynydd Mawr Railway
55020	Bodmin & Wenford Railway
55023	Chinnor & Princes Risborough Railway
55024	Chinnor & Princes Risborough Railway
55025	Long Marston (for sale)
55027	Ecclesbourne Valley Railway
55028	Swanage Railway
55029	Rushden Transport Museum
55031	Eccclesbourne Valley Railway
55032	Wensleydale Railway
55033	Colne Valley Railway
55034	Locomotive Services, Crewe
55508	141108 Colne Valley Railway
55513	141113 Midland Railway Centre
55528	141108 Colne Valley Railway
55533	141113 Midland Railway Centre
56006	Midland Railway Centre
56015	Midland Railway Centre
56055	Cambrian Railway
56057	Strathspey Railway
56062	North Norfolk Railway
56097	Midland Railway Centre
56121	East Lancashire Railway
56160	Denbigh (private)
56169	Helston Railway
56171	Llangollen Railway
56182	North Norfolk Railway
56207	BSC Scunthorpe
56208	Severn Valley Railway
56224	Keith & Dufftown Railway
56271	East Somerset Railway
56274	Wensleydale Railway
56287	Epping & Ongar Railway
56289	East Lancashire Railway
56301	Mid Norfolk Railway
56342	Great Central Railway
56343	Wensleydale Railway
56347	Mid Norfolk Railway
56352	North Norfolk Railway
56356	Barry Island Railway
56358	East Anglian Railway Museum
56408	Spa Valley Railway
56456	Llangollen Railway
56484	Midland Railway Centre
56490	Llangollen Railway
56491	Keith & Dufftown Railway
56492	Dean Forest Railway
56495	Kirklees Light Railway
56505	Swanage Railway
59003	Dartmouth Steam Railway
59004	Dartmouth Steam Railway
59117	Mid Norfolk Railway
59137	East Lancashire Railway
59228	Telford Steam Railway
59245	BSC Scunthorpe
59250	Severn Valley Railway
59276	Great Central Railway
59303	Ecclesbourne Valley Railway
59387	Dean Forest Railway
59404	Bo'ness & Kinneil Railway
59444	Chasewater Railway
59486	Swanage Railway
59488	Dartmouth Steam Railway
59492	Swanage Railway
59493	South Devon Railway
59494	Dartmouth Steam Railway
59500	Wensleydale Railway
59501	Great Central Railway North
59503	Dartmouth Steam Railway
59506	Peak Rail
59507	Dartmouth Steam Railway
59508	Gwili Railway
59509	Wensleydale Railway
59510	Gloucestershire Warwckshire Railway
59511	Strathspey Railway
59513	Dartmouth Steam Railway
59514	Swindon & Cricklade Railway
59515	Yeovil Railway Centre
59517	Dartmouth Steam Railway
59520	Dartmoor Railway
59521	Helston Railway
59522	Nottingham Transport Heritage Trust
59539	North Yorkshire Moors Railway
59575	Great Central Railway
59603	Chasewater Railway
59609	Midland Railway Centre
59659	Midland Railway Centre
59664	Midsomer Norton Railway
59678	West Somerset Railway
59701	East Lancs Railway
59719	Mid Hants Railway

59740	South Devon Railway
59761	Buckinghamshire Railway Centre
59791	Tanat Valley Railway
79018	Ecclesbourne Valley Railway
79443	Bo'ness & Kinneil Railway
79612	Ecclesbourne Valley Railway
79900	Ecclesbourne Valley Railway
79960	Ribble Steam Railway
79962	Keighley & Worth Valley Railway
79963	East Anglian Railway
79964	Keighley & Worth Valley Railway
79976	Nemesis Rail, Burton
79978	Colne Valley Railway
998900	Middleton Railway
999507	Lavender Line

Southern Region DEMU Stock

Class 201, 202, 203 (6S, 6L, 6B)

60000	1001	BR/SR	DMBS	Hastings Diesels Ltd
60001	1001	BR/SR	DMBS	Hastings Diesels Ltd
60016	1012	BR/SR	DMBS	Hastings Diesels Ltd (as 60116)
60018	1013	BR/SR	DMBS	Hastings Diesels Ltd (as 60118)
60019	1013	BR/SR	DMBS	Hastings Diesels Ltd
60500	1001	BR/SR	TS	Hastings Diesels Ltd
60501	1001	BR/SR	TS	Hastings Diesels Ltd
60502	1001	BR/SR	TS	Hastings Diesels Ltd
60527	1013	BR/SR	TS	Hastings Diesels Ltd
60528	1013	BR/SR	TS	Hastings Diesels Ltd
60529	1013	BR/SR	TS	Hastings Diesels Ltd
60700	1001	BR/SR	TF	Hastings Diesels Ltd
60708	1012	BR/SR	TF	Hastings Diesels Ltd
60709	1013	BR/SR	TF	Hastings Diesels Ltd
60750	1032	BR/SR	TBUF	Hastings Diesels Ltd (ex Departmental)

Class 205 (2H, 3H)

60108	1109	BR/SR	DMBSO	Eden Valley Railway
60110	1111	BR/SR	DMBSO	Epping & Ongar Railway
60117	1118	BR/SR	DMBSO	Lavender Line
60122	1123	BR/SR	DMBSO	Lavender Line
60124	1125	BR/SR	DMBSO	Mid Hants Railway
60146	1128	BR/SR	DMBSO	Dartmoor Railway
60150	1132	BR/SR	DMBSO	Dartmoor Railway
60151	1133	BR/SR	DMBSO	Lavender Line
60154	1101	BR/SR	DMBSO	East Kent Railway
60658	1109	BR/SR	TSO	Eden Valley Railway
60669	1120	BR/SR	TSO	Swindon & Cricklade Railway
60673	1128	BR/SR	TSO	Dartmoor Railway
60677	1132	BR/SR	TSO	Dartmoor Railway
60678	1133	BR/SR	TSO	Lavender Line
60800	1101	BR/SR	DTC	East Kent Railway
60808	1109	BR/SR	DTC	Eden Valley Railway
60810	1111	BR/SR	DTS	Epping & Ongar Railway
60820	1121	BR/SR	DTC	Lavender Line
60822	1123	BR/SR	DTC	Swindon & Cricklade Railway
60824	1125	BR/SR	DTC	Mid Hants Railway
60827	1128	BR/SR	DTC	Dartmoor Railway
60828	1118	BR/SR	DTC	Lavender Line
60830	1131	BR/SR	DTC	Lavender Line
60831	1132	BR/SR	DTC	Dartmoor Railway
60832	1133	BR/SR	DTC	Lavender Line

Class 207 (3D)

60127	1302	BR/SR	DMBS	Swindon & Cricklade Railway
60130	1305	BR/SR	DMBS	East Lancs Railway
60142	1317	BR/SR	DMBS	Spa Valley Railway
60616	1317	BR/SR	TC	Spa Valley Railway
60904	1305	BR/SR	DTS	East Lancs Railway
60916	1317	BR/SR	DTS	Spa Valley Railway

Preserved Modern Traction - Electric Multiple Unit Stock

Unclassified

3267		LNER	DMBL	Percy Main (National Railway Museum owned)
8143		LNWR	DMBS	National Railway Museum York
117		MSJ&AR	T	Midland Railway Centre
121		MSJ&AR	T	Midland Railway Centre
79998	-	BR/ScR	DMBS	Milton of Crathes (Battery set)
79999	-	BR/ScR	DTC	Milton of Crathes (Battery set)

5BEL

279	3051	SR	TFK	5-BEL Trust
281	3053	SR	TFK	VSOE Stewarts Lane
280	3052	SR	TFK	VSOE Stewarts Lane
282	3051	SR	TFK	5-BEL Trust
283	3053	SR	TFK	VSOE Stewarts Lane
284	3052	SR	TFK	VSOE Stewarts Lane
285	3053	SR	TPT	5-BEL Trust
286	3051	SR	TPT	VSOE Stewarts Lane
287	3052	SR	TPT	5-BEL Trust
288	3051	SR	DMBPT	5-BEL Trust
289	3051	SR	DMBPT	Little Mill Inn, Rowarth, Derbyshire
291	3052	SR	DMBPT	5-BEL Trust
292	3053	SR	DMBPT	VSOE Stewarts Lane
293	3053	SR	DMBPT	VSOE Stewarts Lane

6PUL

264	3012	SR	TKC	VSOE Stewarts Lane
278	3017	SR	TKC	VSOE Stewarts Lane

2BIL (Class 401)

10656	2090	SR	DMBS	National Railway Museum Shildon
12123	2090	SR	DTC	National Railway Museum Shildon

4COR (Class 404)

10096	3142	SR	TSK	East Kent Railway
11161	3142	SR	DMBS	Sellinge
11179	3131	SR	DMBS	National Railway Museum York
11187	3135	SR	DMBS	East Kent Railway
11201	3142	SR	DMBS	Sellinge
11825	3142	SR	TC	Sellinge

4DD

13003	4002	SR	DMBT	Sellinge
13004	4002	SR	DMBT	Northampton Ironstone Railway

AM2 (Class 302)

75033	302201	BR/ER	DTSO	Mangapps Farm
75250	302277	BR/ER	DTSO	Mangapps Farm

AM3 (Class 303)

61503	303023	BR/ScR	MBS	Bo'ness & Kinneil Railway
75597	303032	BR/ScR	DTSO	Bo'ness & Kinneil Railway
75632	303032	BR/ScR	BDTSO	Bo'ness & Kinneil Railway

AM6 (Class 306)

65217	306017	BR/ER	DMSO	National Railway Museum, Shildon
65417	306017	BR/ER	TBC	National Railway Museum, Shildon
65617	306017	BR/ER	DTSO	National Railway Museum, Shildon

AM7 (Class 307)

75023	307123	BR/ER	DTBSO	Coulsdon Historic Vehicles, Finmere

AM8 (Class 308)

75881	308136	BR/ER	DTCO	Coulsdon Historic Vehicles, Finmere

AM9 (Class 309)

61928	309624	BR/ER	MBSO	Lavender Line
61937	309616	BR/ER	MBSO	Tanat Valley Railway
75642	309616	BR/ER	BDTC	Tanat Valley Railway
75965	309624	BR/ER	BDTC	Lavender Line
75972	309624	BR/ER	DTSO	Lavender Line
75981	309616	BR/ER	DTSO	Tanat Valley Railway

AM11 (Class 311)

62174	311103	BR/ScR	MBSO	Summerlee
76433	311103	BR/ScR	DTSO	Summerlee

AM12 (Class 312)

71205	312792	BR/ER	TS	Colne Valley Railway
78037	312792	BR/ER	DTS	Colne Valley Railway

Class 370

M49006	APT	BR/LMR	M	Crewe Heritage Centre

Class 373 (Eurostar)

3101		Eurostar	DM (only)	Training vehicle at Doncaster Academy
3102		Eurostar	DM (only)	Training vehicle at Birmingham Training Academy
3106		Eurostar	DM, plus car 9	Train World, Brussels
3308		Eurostar	DM (only)	National Railway Museum, York

4 SUB (Class 405)

8143	4308	SR	DMBS	National Railway Museum, York
10239	4732	BR/SR	TS	Loco Storage Ltd, Margate
12354	4732	BR/SR	TSO	Loco Storage Ltd, Margate
12795	4732	BR/SR	DMBS	Loco Storage Ltd, Margate
12796	4732	BR/SR	DMBS	Loco Storage Ltd, Margate

4CEP/BEP (Class 411/412)

61229	1537	BR/SR	DMBSO	Eastleigh Works
61230	1537	BR/SR	DMBSO	Eastleigh Works
61736	1198	BR/SR	DMBSO	Chinnor & Princess Risborough Railway
61737	1198	BR/SR	DMBSO	Chinnor & Princess Risborough Railway
61742	1589	BR/SR	DMBSO	Dartmoor Railway
61743	1589	BR/SR	DMBSO	Dartmoor Railway
61798	2315	BR/SR	DMBSO	Eden Valley Railway
61799	2315	BR/SR	DMBSO	Eden Valley Railway
61804	2311	BR/SR	DMBSO	Eden Valley Railway
61805	2311	BR/SR	DMBSO	Eden Valley Railway
69013	7012	BR/SR	TBS	Epping and Ongar Railway
70229	2315	BR/SR	TSO	Eden Valley Railway
70235	7107	BR/SR	TBCK	Epping and Ongar Railway
70262	1524	BR/SR	TSO	Hastings Diesels Ltd
70284	1520	BR/SR	TSO	Northampton Ironstone Railway
70292	1554	BR/SR	TSO	Speyside Railway, Grantown
70296	1559	BR/SR	TSO	Northampton Ironstone Railway
70300	1698	BR/SR	TSO	Fighting Cocks Pub, Middleton St George
70345	1500	BR/SR	TBCK	Hydraulic House, Sutton Bridge, Cambridgeshire
70354	2315	BR/SR	TBCK	Eden Valley Railway
70510	1597	BR/SR	TSO	Northampton Ironstone Railway
70527	1589	BR/SR	TSO	Great Central Railway
70531	1610	BR/SR	TSO	Speyside Railway, Grantown
70539	2311	BR/SR	TBCK	Eden Valley Railway
70547	1569	BR/SR	TSO	Private in Hungerford
70549	1567	BR/SR	TSO	East Lancs Railway
70573	1198	BR/SR	TBCK	Chinnor & Princess Risborough Railway
70576	1589	BR/SR	TBCK	Great Central Railway
70607	2311	BR/SR	TSO	Eden Valley Railway

2HAP (Class 414)

61275	4308	BR/SR	DMBS	National Railway Museum, Shildon
61287	4311	BR/SR	DMBS	AB Loco, Peak Rail, Darley Dale

75395	4308	BR/SR	DTC	National Railway Museum, Shildon
75407	4311	BR/SR	DTS	AB Loco, Peak Rail, Darley Dale

4EPB (Class 415)

14351	5176	BR/SR	DMBSO	Northampton Ironstone Railway
14352	5176	BR/SR	DMBSO	Loco Storage Ltd, Margate
15354	5176	BR/SR	TSO	Northampton Ironstone Railway
15396	5176	BR/SR	TSO	Northampton Ironstone Railway

2EPB (Class 416)

14573	6307	BR/SR	DMBS	Hope Farm, Sellindge
16117	6307	BR/SR	DTS	Hope Farm, Sellindge
65321	5791	BR/SR	DMBS	Peak Rail, Darley Dale
65373	5759	BR/SR	DMBS	Southall
77112	5793	BR/SR	DTS	Peak Rail, Darley Dale
77558	5759	BR/SR	DTS	Southall

MLV (Class 419)

68001	9001	BR/SR	DMBL	Epping and Ongar Railway
68002	9002	BR/SR	DMBL	Southall
68003	9003	BR/SR	DMBL	Eden Valley Railway
68004	9004	BR/SR	DMBL	Mid-Norfolk Railway
68005	9005	BR/SR	DMBL	Eden Valley Railway
68008	9008	BR/SR	DMBL	Southall
68009	9009	BR/SR	DMBL	Southall
68010	9010	BR/SR	DMBL	Eden Valley Railway

4CIG (Class 421)

62043	1753	BR/SR	MBSO	Finmere
62287	1303	BR/SR	MBSO	Lincolnshire Wolds Railway
62385	1399	BR/SR	MBSO	East Kent Railway
62402	1497	BR/SR	MBSO	Spa Valley Railway
70721	1753	BR/SR	TSO	Finmere
71041	1306	BR/SR	TSO	Private in Hever
71080	1881	BR/SR	TSO	Dean Forest Railway
71085	1884	BR/SR	TSO	Private in Kent
76048	1753	BR/SR	DTC	Finmere
76102	1753	BR/SR	DTC	Finmere
76740	1392	BR/SR	DTC	Southall
76747	1399	BR/SR	DTC	Dartmoor Railway
76764	1497	BR/SR	DTC	Spa Valley Railway
76835	1497	BR/SR	DTC	Spa Valley Railway

4BIG (Class 422)

69302	2251	BR/SR	TRSB	Abbey View Centre, Neath
69304	2260	BR/SR	TRSB	Northampton Ironstone Railway
69306	2254	BR/SR	TRSB	Spa Valley Railway
69310	2255	BR/SR	TRSB	Dartmoor Railway
69316	2258	BR/SR	TRSB	Waverley Heritage Centre
69318	2259	BR/SR	TRSB	Colne Valley Railway
69332	2257	BR/SR	TRSB	Dartmoor Railway
69333	2262	BR/SR	TRSB	Lavender Line
69335	2209	BR/SR	TRSB	Wensleydale Railway
69337	2210	BR/SR	TRSB	Hastings Diesels Ltd
69339	2205	BR/SR	TRSB	Finmere

4VEP/VOP (Class 423)

62236	3417	BR/SR	MBSO	Bluebell Railway
70797	3417	BR/SR	TSO	Bluebell Railway
70904	3905	BR/SR	TSO	East Kent Railway
76262	3417	BR/SR	DTCO	Bluebell Railway
76263	3417	BR/SR	DTCO	Bluebell Railway
76397	3905	BR/SR	DTC	East Kent Railway
76398	3905	BR/SR	DTC	East Kent Railway
76875	3545	BR/SR	DTC	East Kent Railway

76887	3568	BR/SR	DTC	Woking Miniature Railway

4TC (Class 438)

70823	428	BR/SR	TBSK	London Transport set
70824	413	BR/SR	TBSK	Swanage Railway
70826	415	BR/SR	TBSK	Sandford & Barnwell Station
70855	412	BR/SR	TFK	Swanage Railway
70859	416	BR/SR	TFK	Stravithie Station
70860	417	BR/SR	TFK	Darlington North Road
71163	428	BR/SR	TFK	London Transport set
76275	404	BR/SR	DTSO	Swanage Railway
76277	405	BR/SR	DTSO	Dartmoor Railway
76297	428	BR/SR	DTSO	London Transport set
76298	415	BR/SR	DTSO	Swanage Railway
76301	417	BR/SR	DTSO	Bellingham, Northumberland
76302	417	BR/SR	DTSO	Bellingham, Northumberland
76322	427	BR/SR	DTSO	Swanage Railway
76324	428	BR/SR	DTSO	London Transport set

Class 457

67300	7001	BR/WR	DMSO	East Kent Railway

1940 Waterloo & City (Class 487)

61		SR	DMSO	LT Museum, Acton

GLV (Class 489)

68500	9101	BR/IC	DMBL	Ecclesbourne Valley Railway
68503	9104	BR/IC	DMBL	Spa Valley Railway
68506	9106	BR/IC	DMBL	Ecclesbourne Valley Railway
68507	9108	BR/IC	DMBL	Great Central Railway
68509	9110	BR/IC	DMBL	Vale of Glamorgan Railway

Class 501

61183	501183	BR/LM	DMBS	Coulsdon Historic Vehicles, Finmere
75186	501183	BR/LM	DTBS	Coulsdon Historic Vehicles, Finmere

Class 502

28361		LMS	DMBS	Burscough
29896		LMS	DTC	Burscough

Class 503

28690		LMS	DMBS	Loco Services, Margate
29282		LMS	DTS	Loco Services, Margate
29720		LMS	TCO	Loco Services, Margate

Class 504

65451	-	BR/LM	DMBSO	East Lancs Railway
77172	-	BR/LM	DTBSO	East Lancs Railway

Class 390 (APT)

SC49006	-	BR	MC	Railway Age Crewe

Right: *London Transport own one former BR Southern Region/NSE 4TC set, formed of vehicles DTSO 76297 and 76324 with TBSK 70823 and TFK 71163. The set, painted in London Transport red livery is usually kept at one of the LUL surface stock depots, but is available for charter train and special use. The set with vehicle No. 70823 featured, is seen on the Swanage Railway.* **Antony Christie**

Above: *In addition to major railways owning locomotives, a number are owned by small groups or even individuals, who have funded major restoration projects to see 'their' loco return to traffic. Class 37 No. 37227 is one such loco, owned by a small group of dedicated enthusiasts the loco has been restored to front line condition and is presently operating on the Chinnor and Princess Risborough Railway. It displays Railfreight Metals sub-sector livery.* **Russell Watkins**

Left Middle: *Small shunting locos are always very useful to preserved railways, where at the turn of a switch a loco is quickly available for pilotage work. With the reducing need for such locos with the main freight operators, a huge number have become available. Class 09 No. 09024, displaying BR General grey livery , a dual braked loco, works on the East Lancs Railway at Bury.* **Antony Christie**

Left Lower: *Class 25 No. 25278 (D7628) owned by the North Yorkshire Moors Railway holds a certificate to operate limited services over Network Rail line between Grosmont and Whitby. This allowing the provision of a through service between Network Rail and the NYMR. The loco is seen at Whitby.* **Antony Christie**

Above: *Displaying BR black livery with Lion and Wheel cab side logo and numbers in white, Class 03 No. D2059 is seen working on the Isle of Wight Railway, powering a vintage collection of Island stock.* **Antony Christie**

Right Middle: *A loco which in 2018 returned to the main line, operating with Locomotive Services based at Crewe is Class 40 No. D213 (40013). Privately owned the loco has now been restored to full main line condition and displays BR green livery with a small yellow warning end. No. D213 is seen working on the East Lancs Railway.* **Antony Christie**

Right Lower: *A sizeable number of first generation Diesel Mechanical Multiple Units (DMMUs) are in operation on preserved railways. Many have been returned to their 1950s/1960s condition displaying various guises of green livery. This two car set of Metro-Cammell vehicle Nos. 51192 and 56352 are seen at Sheringham on the North Norfolk Railway. This twin-set is actually owned by the National Railway Museum, York and on loan to the railway.* **Antony Christie**

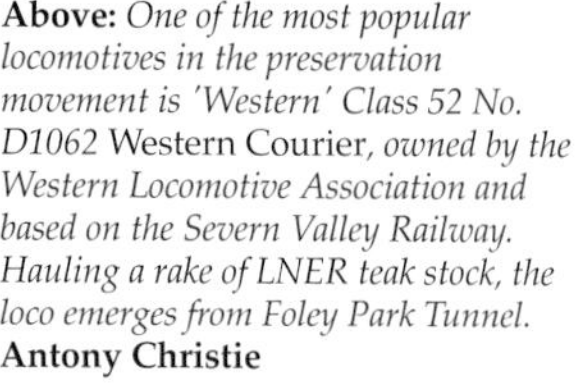

Above: *One of the most popular locomotives in the preservation movement is 'Western' Class 52 No. D1062* Western Courier, *owned by the Western Locomotive Association and based on the Severn Valley Railway. Hauling a rake of LNER teak stock, the loco emerges from Foley Park Tunnel.* **Antony Christie**

Left Middle: *A large number of Type 1 0-6-0 diesel-hydraulic Class 14 locomotives are in preservation, mostly due to the industrial sector taking the locos from BR when they were withdrawn when almost new. No. D9521 now operates on the Dean Forest Railway and is seen with a LMS Brake van and an industrial shunter at Norchard.* **Antony Christie**

Left Lower: *The Scottish Railway Preservation Society at Bo'ness have restored a three-car Class 126 set to immaculate 1960s BR green livery with whisker ends - vehicles Nos. 51017, 59404 and 51043. The three car set is seen at Bo'ness.* **Antony Christie**

Above: *Immaculately restored Class 117 DMBS No. 51384 is seen paired with former Class 121 driving Trailer Composite No. W56287. These vehicles are usually based on the Colne Valley Railway, but are seen on the Epping and Ongar Railway.* **Antony Christie**

Left Middle: *Used by Chiltern Railways until recently, Class 121 'Bubble' No. 55020 (121020) is now preserved on the Bodmin and Wenford Railway in Cornwall. Still sporting Chiltern blue livery, the vehicle is seen approaching Bodmin Parkway station, the interchange with the National network.* **Antony Christie**

Left Lower: *The former BR Research Derby RTC-based Class 901 No. 901002 formed of vehicles 977693 and 977694, has now been rebuilt to a Class 101 passenger set and operated on the Barry Tourist Railway. Painted in green livery the set still sports an end power jumper and headlight from its departmental days. The set is now numbered as 50222 and 50338 their original numbers.* **Antony Christie**

Above: *With the UKs largest railfreight operator DB removing the need for small shunting locos and deploying main line locos to perform shunting and train make up work, a number of good quality Class 08 became available for sale. This included Bescot-allocated No. 08907, carrying DB red livery. The loco is now preserved at the Great Central Railway, Loughborough.* **Antony Christie**

Below: *Class 25 No. D7535 (25185), restored to BR 1960s Rail Blue with a small yellow bib front end has for some time been based on the Paignton and Dartmouth Railway, where this illustration was recorded. However, in autumn 2018 a swap was made with Class 37 No. 37275 and the Class 25 is now allocated to the South Devon Railway.* **Antony Christie**

Right Upper: *BRCW Type 2 Class 26 No. 26038* Tom Clift *is currently operating on the North Yorkshire Moors Railway, rather than its usual base at Bo'ness. The loco, reported to have been one of the highest mileage preserved diesels in 2017-2018, is seen at Grosmont.* **Antony Christie**

Right Middle: *One of the big problems with preserving electric multiple units is the general inability to operate them under their own power, as the provision of overhead or third rail supplies at a preserved railway would both be too expensive and too dangerous. Class 303 'Glasgow Blue Train' No. 303032 is preserved at the Bo'ness & Kinneil Railway.* **Antony Christie**

Below: *Electric train Supply (ETS) fitted Class 47/4 No. 47579* James Nightall GC *is owned by Mangapps Farm Museum, but has recently been working on the Mid Hants Railway (Watercress Line), where this illustration shows the loco in large logo blue livery.* **Antony Christie**

Preserved Steam Locomotives

Great Western

and constitute companies

No.	Name	Class	Wheel Arrangement	Location
426			0-6-2T	Keighley & Worth Valley Rly
450			0-6-2T	NRM at Gwili Railway
813			0-6-0ST	Severn Valley Railway
1338			0-6-0ST	Didcot Railway Centre
1340	*Trojan*		0-6-0ST	Didcot Railway Centre
1363		1361	0-6-0ST	Didcot Railway Centre
1369		1366	0-6-0PT	South Devon Railway
1420		1400	0-4-2T	South Devon Railway
1442		1400	0-4-2T	Tiverton Museum
1450		1400	0-4-2T	Severn Valley Railway
1466		1400	0-4-2T	Dean Forest Railway
1501		1500	0-6-0PT	Severn Valley Railway
1638		1600	0-6-0PT	Kent & East Sussex Railway
2516		Dean Goods	0-6-0	Swindon Museum, Swindon
2807		2800	2-8-0	Gloucestershire Warwickshire Railway
2818		2800	2-8-0	Steam, Swindon
2857		2800	2-8-0	Severn Valley Railway
2859		2800	2-8-0	Private in Congleton
2861		2800	2-8-0	Barry
2873		2800	2-8-0	South Devon Railway (parts for 3803)
2874		2800	2-8-0	Gloucestershire Warwickshire Railway
2885		2800	2-8-0	Tyseley
3205		2251	0-6-0	South Devon Railway
3440	*City of Truro*	City	4-4-0	Steam Museum, Swindon
3650		5700	0-6-0PT	Didcot Railway Centre
3738		5700	0-6-0PT	Didcot Railway Centre
3802		2800	2-8-0	Llangollen Railway
3803		2800	2-8-0	South Devon Railway
3814		2800	2-8-0	Llangollen Railway
3822		2800	2-8-0	Gloucestershire Warwickshire Railway
3845		2800	2-8-0	West Somerset Railway
3850		2800	2-8-0	Gloucestershire Warwickshire Railway
3855		2800	2-8-0	East Lancs Railway
3862		2800	2-8-0	Northampton & Lamport
4003	*Lode Star*	Star	4-6-0	National Railway Museum York
4073	*Caerphilly Castle*	Castle	4-6-0	Steam Museum, Swindon
4079	*Pendennis Castle*	Castle	4-6-0	Didcot Railway Centre
4110		5101	2-6-2T	West Somerset Railway
4115		5101	2-6-2T	Didcot Railway Centre
4121		5101	2-6-2T	Tyseley Museum
4141		5101	2-6-2T	Epping and Ongar Railway
4144		5101	2-6-2T	Didcot Railway Centre
4150		5101	2-6-2T	Severn Valley Railway
4160		5101	2-6-2T	Llangollen Railway
4247		4200	2-8-0T	Bodmin & Wenford
4248		4200	2-8-0T	Steam Museum, Swindon
4253		4200	2-8-0T	Kent & East Sussex Railway
4270		4200	2-8-0T	Gloucestershire Warwickshire Railway
4277		4200	2-8-0T	Dartmouth Steam Railway
4555	*Warrior*	4500	2-6-2T	Dartmouth Steam Railway
4561		4500	2-6-2T	West Somerset Railway
4566		4500	2-6-2T	Severn Valley Railway
4588		4500	2-6-2T	Tyseley Museum
4612		5700	0-6-0PT	Bodmin & Wenford Railway
4920	*Dumbleton Hall*	Hall	4-6-0	South Devon Railway
4930	*Hagley Hall*	Hall	4-6-0	Severn Valley Railway
4936	*Kinlet Hall*	Hall	4-6-0	Tyseley Museum
4953	*Pitchford Hall*	Hall	4-6-0	Epping and Ongar Railway

4965	*Rood Ashton Hall*	Hall	4-6-0	Tyseley Museum
4979	*Wootton Hall*	Hall	4-6-0	Ribble Steam Railway
5029	*Nunney Castle*	Castle	4-6-0	Didcot Railway Centre
5043	*Earl of Mt Edgecumbe*	Castle	4-6-0	Tyseley Museum
5051	*Earl Bathurst*	Castle	4-6-0	Didcot Railway Centre
5080	*Defiant*	Castle	4-6-0	Tyseley Museum
5164		5101	2-6-2T	Barrow Hill
5193		5101	2-6-2T	West Somerset Rly (rebuilt as Mogul 9351)
5199		5101	2-6-2T	Llangollen Railway
5224		5205	2-8-0T	West Somerset Railway
5227		5205	2-8-0T	Barry
5239	*Goliath*	5205	2-8-0T	Dartmouth Steam Railway
5322		4300	2-8-0T	Didcot Railway Centre
5521		4500	2-6-2T	Avon Valley Railway
5526		4500	2-6-2T	South Devon Railway
5532		4500	2-6-2T	Llangollen Railway
5538		4500	2-6-2T	Flower Mill
5539		4500	2-6-2T	Barry Railway
5541		4500	2-6-2T	Dean Forest Railway
5542		4500	2-6-2T	South Devon Railway
5552		4500	2-6-2T	Bodmin & Wenford Railway
5553		4500	2-6-2T	Peak Rail
5572		4500	2-6-2T	Didcot Railway Centre
5619		5600	0-6-2T	Midland Railway Centre
5637		5600	0-6-2T	East Somerset Railway
5643		5600	0-6-2T	Embsay and Bolton Abbey
5668		5600	0-6-2T	Kent & East Sussex Railway
5764		5700	0-6-0PT	Severn Valley Railway
5775		5700	0-6-0PT	Keighley & Worth Valley Railway
5786		5700	0-6-0PT	South Devon Railway as L92
5900	*Hinderton Hall*	Hall	4-6-0	Didcot Railway Centre
5952	*Cogan Hall*	Hall	4-6-0	Llangollen Railway
5967	*Bickmarsh Hall*	Hall	4-6-0	Northampton & Lamport
5972	*Olton Hall*	Hall	4-6-0	Carnforth
6000	*King George V*	King	4-6-0	Swindon Museum, Swindon
6023	*King Edward II*	King	4-6-0	Didcot Railway Centre
6024	*King Edward I*	King	4-6-0	West Somerset Railway (GWS)
6106		6100	2-6-2T	Didcot Railway Centre
6412		6400	0-6-0PT	South Devon Railway
6430		6400	0-6-0PT	Llangollen Railway
6435		6400	0-6-0PT	Bodmin & Wenford
6619		5600	0-6-2T	Kent & East Sussex Railway
6634		5600	0-6-2T	Peak Rail
6686		5600	0-6-2T	Barry
6695		5600	0-6-2T	West Somerset Railway
6697		5600	0-6-2T	Didcot Railway Centre
6960	*RaveninghamHall*	Mod Hall	4-6-0	West Somerset Railway
6984	*Owsden Hall*	Mod Hall	4-6-0	Severn Valley Railway
6989	*Wightwick Hall*	Mod Hall	4-6-0	Quainton Road
6990	*Witherslack Hall*	Mod Hall	4-6-0	Great Central Railway
6998	*Burton Agnes Hall*	Mod Hall	4-6-0	Didcot Railway Centre
7027	*Thornbury Castle*	Castle	4-6-0	West Somerset Railway
7029	*Clun Castle*	Castle	4-6-0	Tyseley Museum
7200		7200	2-8-2T	Quainton Road
7202		7200	2-8-2T	Didcot Railway Centre
7229		7200	2-8-2T	East Lancs Railway
7325		4300	2-6-0	Severn Valley Railway
7714		5700	0-6-0PT	Severn Valley Railway
7715		5700	0-6-0PT	Quainton Road as L99
7752		5700	0-6-0PT	Tyseley Museum
7754		5700	0-6-0PT	Llangollen Railway
7760		5700	0-6-0PT	Tyseley Museum
7802	*Bradley Manor*	Manor	4-6-0	Severn Valley Railway
7808	*Cookham Manor*	Manor	4-6-0	Didcot Railway Centre
7812	*Erlestoke Manor*	Manor	4-6-0	Tyseley Museum
7819	*Hinton Manor*	Manor	4-6-0	Severn Valley Railway

7820	*Dinmore Manor*	Manor	4-6-0	GWR
7821	*Ditcheat Manor*	Manor	4-6-0	Retail Park, Swindon
7822	*Foxcote Manor*	Manor	4-6-0	Steam Museum, Swindon
7827	*Lydham Manor*	Manor	4-6-0	Dartmouth Steam Railway
7828	*Odney Manor*	Manor	4-6-0	West Somerset Railway
7903	*Foremarke Hall*	Mod Hall	4-6-0	GWR
7927	*Willington Hall*	Mod Hall	4-6-0	Llangollen Railway
9017	*Earl of Berkeley*	Dukedog	4-4-0	Bluebell Railway
9351		(rebuild)	2-6-0	West Somerset Railway
9400		9400	0-6-0PT	Steam Museum, Swindon
9466		9400	0-6-0PT	Quainton Road
9600		5700	0-6-0PT	Tyseley Museum
9629		5700	0-6-0PT	Pontypool & Blaenavon
9642		5700	0-6-0PT	GWR
9681		5700	0-6-0PT	Dean Forest Railway
9682		5700	0-6-0PT	Dean Forest Railway

Southern
and constitute companies

No.	Name	Class	Wheel Arrangement	Location
W24	*Calbourne*	O2	0-4-4T	IoW Steam Railway
30053		M7	0-4-4T	Swanage Railway
30064		USA	0-6-0T	Bluebell Railway
30065		USA	0-6-0T	Kent & East Sussex Railway
30070 (DS238)		USA	0-6-0T	Kent & East Sussex Railway
30072		USA	0-6-0T	Keighley & Worth Valley Railway
30075		USA	0-6-0T	Mid-Hants Railway (Yugoslav loco)
30076		USA	0-6-0T	Mid-Hants Railway (Yugoslav loco)
30096	*Normandy*	B4	0-4-0T	Bluebell Railway
30102	*Granville*	B4	0-4-0T	Bressingham
30120		T9	4-4-0	Swanage Railway
30245		M7	0-4-4T	National Railway Museum
30499		S15	4-6-0	Mid Hants Railway
30506		S15	4-6-0	Mid-Hants Railway
30541		Q	0-6-0	Bluebell Railway
30583		0415	4-4-2T	Bluebell Railway
30585		0298	2-4-0WT	Quainton
30587		0298	2-4-0WT	NRM at Bodmin & Wenford
30777	*Sir Lamiel*	N15	4-6-0	Great Central Railway
30825		S15	4-6-0	North Yorkshire Moors Railway
30828		S15	4-6-0	Mid-Hants Railway
30830		S15	4-6-0	North Yorkshire Moors Railway
30847		S15	4-6-0	Bluebell Railway
30850	*Lord Nelson*	LN	4-6-0	Mid-Hants Railway
30925	*Cheltenham*	V	4-4-0	Mid-Hants Railway
30926	*Repton*	V	4-4-0	North Yorkshire Moors Railway
30928	*Stowe*	V	4-4-0	Bluebell Railway
31027		P	0-6-0T	Bluebell Railway
31065 (65)		O1	0-6-0	Bluebell Railway
31178		P1	0-6-0T	Bluebell Railway
31263		H	0-4-4T	Bluebell Railway
31323 (323)		P	0-6-0T	Bluebell Railway
31556		P	0-6-0T	Kent & East Sussex Railway
31592		C	0-6-0	Bluebell Railway
31618		U	2-6-0	Bluebell Railway
31625		U	2-6-0	Swanage Railway
31638		U	2-6-0	Bluebell Railway
31737		D	4-4-0	National Railway Museum York
31806		U	2-6-0	Swanage Railway
31874		N	2-6-0	Swanage Railway
32110	*Cannock Wood*	E1	0-6-0T	Isle of White Railway
32473	*Birch Grove*	E4	0-6-2T	Bluebell Railway
32636	*Fenchurch*	A1X	0-6-0T	Bluebell Railway

32640 W11	*Newport*	A1X	0-6-0T	IoW Steam Railway
32646	*Freshwater*	A1X	0-6-0T	IoW Steam Railwau
32650	*Whitechapel*	A1X	0-6-0T	Spa Valley Railway
32654	*Waddon*	A1X	0-6-0T	Canadian Railway Museum
32655	*Stepney*	A1X	0-6-0T	Bluebell Railway
32662	*Martello*	A1X	0-6-0T	Bressingham
32670	*Poplar*	A1X	0-6-0T	Kent & East Sussex Railway
32672	*Fenchurch*	A1X	0-6-0T	Bluebell Railway
32678	*Knowle*	A1X	0-6-0T	Kent & East Sussex Railway
32682	*Boxhill*	A1X	0-6-0T	National Railway Museum
33001		Q1	0-6-0	National Railway Museum
34007	*Wadebridge*	WC	4-6-2	Mid-Hants Railway
34010	*Sidmouth*	WC	4-6-2	Swanage Railway
34016	*Bodmin*	WC	4-6-2	WCRC Carnforth
34023	*Blackmore Vale*	WC	4-6-2	Bluebell Railway
34027	*Taw Valley*	WC	4-6-2	Severn Valley Railway
34028	*Eddystone*	WC	4-6-2	Swanage Railway
34039	*Boscastle*	WC	4-6-2	Great Central Railway
34046	*Braunton*	WC	4-6-2	Southall
34051	*Winston Churchill*	BB	4-6-2	National Railway Museum York
34053	*Sir Keith Park*	BB	4-6-2	Swanage Railway
34058	*Sir Frederick Pile*	BB	4-6-2	Midland Railway Centre
34059	*Sir Archibald Sinclair*	BB	4-6-2	Bluebell Railway
34067	*Tangmere*	BB	4-6-2	WCRC Carnforth
34070	*Manston*	BB	4-6-2	Swanage Railway
34072	*257 Squadron*	BB	4-6-2	Swanage Railway
34073	*249 Squadron*	BB	4-6-2	East Lancs Railway
34081	*92 Squadron*	BB	4-6-2	North Norfolk Railway
34092	*City of Wells*	WC	4-6-2	East Lancs Railway
34101	*Hartland*	WC	4-6-2	North Yorkshire Moors Railway
34105	*Swanage*	WC	4-6-2	Mid-Hants Railway
35005	*Canadian Pacific*	MN	4-6-2	Mid-Hants Railway
35006	*Peninsular & Oriental S. N Co*	MN	4-6-2	Gloucestershire Warwickshire Railway
35009	*Shaw Savill*	MN	4-6-2	East Lancs Railway
35010	*Blue Star*	MN	4-6-2	Colne Valley Railway
35011	*General Steam Navigation*	MN	4-6-2	Sellinge (restoration)
35018	*British India Line*	MN	4-6-2	WCRC Carnforth
35022	*Holland America Line*	MN	4-6-2	Private at Bury
35025	*Brocklebamk Line*	MN	4-6-2	Private at Sellindge
35027	*Port Line*	MN	4-6-2	Private in Bury
35028	*Clan Line*	MN	4-6-2	Stewarts Lane
35029	*Ellerman Lines*	MN	4-6-2	National Railway Museum York
B110		E1	0-6-0T	East Somerset Railway
214	*Gladstone*	B	0-4-0	National Railway Museum York
563		T3	4-4-0	Flower Mill/Swanage

London Midland Scottish
and constitute companies

No.	Name	Class	Wheel Arrangement	Location
790	*Hardwicke*	LNWR	2-4-0	National Railway Museum York
1000		MC	4-4-0	NRM at Barrow Hill
1719	*Lady Nan*		0-4-0ST	East Somerset Railway
3020	*Cornwall*	LNWR	2-2-2	NRM at Buckingham Railway
16379		GSWR	0-6-0T	Glasgow Museum
41241		Class 2	2-6-2T	Keighley & Worth Valley Railway
41298		Class 2	2-6-2T	Isle of Wight Railway
41312		Class 2	2-6-2T	Mid-Hants Railway
41313		Class 2	2-6-2T	Isle of Wight Railway
41708		1F	0-6-0T	Barrow Hill
41966	*Thundersley*		4-4-2T	Bressingham
42073			2-6-4T	Lakeside and Haverthwaite Railway

42085			2-6-4T	Lakeside and Haverthwaite Railway
42500			2-6-4T	National Railway Museum
42700		Crab	2-6-0	National Railway Museum
42765		Crab	2-6-0	East Lancs Railway
42859		Crab	2-6-0	RAF Binbrook
42968		Crab	2-6-0	Severn Valley Railway
43106		4MT	2-6-0	Severn Valley Railway
43924		4F	0-6-0	Keighley & Worth Valley Railway
44027		4F	0-6-0	Vale of Berkley Railway
44123		4F	0-6-0	Avon Valley Railway
44422		4F	0-6-0	West Somerset Railway
44767	*George Stephenson*	Black 5	4-6-0	WCRC Carnforth
44806	*Kenneth Aldcroft*	Black 5	4-6-0	North Yorkshire Moors Railway
44871	*Sovereign*	Black 5	4-6-0	East Lancs Railway
44901		Black 5	4-6-0	Vale of Berkeley Railway
44932		Black 5	4-6-0	Carnforth
45000		Black 5	4-6-0	National Railway Museum, Shildon
45025		Black 5	4-6-0	Strathspey Railway
45110	*RAF Biggin Hill*	Black 5	4-6-0	Severn Valley Railway
45163		Black 5	4-6-0	Churnet Valley Railway
45212		Black 5	4-6-0	Keighley & Worth Valley Railway
45231	*The Sherwood Forester*	Black 5	4-6-0	Crewe
45293		Black 5	4-6-0	Churnet Valley Railway
45305		Black 5	4-6-0	Great Central Railway
45337		Black 5	4-6-0	Llangollen Railway
45379		Black 5	4-6-0	Loco Storage, Margate
45407	*Lancashire Fusilier*	Black 5	4-6-0	East Lancs Railway
45428	*Eric Treacy*	Black 5	4-6-0	North Yorkshire Moors Railway
45491		Black 5	4-6-0	Great Central Railway
45593	*Kolhapur*	Jubilee	4-6-0	Tyseley Museum
45596	*Bahamas*	Jubilee	4-6-0	Tyseley Museum
45690	*Leander*	Jubilee	4-6-0	WCRC Carnforth
45699	*Galatea*	Jubilee	4-6-0	WCRC Carnforth
46100	*Royal Scot*	Royal Scot	4-6-0	Southall
46115	*Scots Guardsman*	Royal Scot	4-6-0	Carnforth
46201	*Princess Elizabeth*	Princess	4-6-2	Carnforth
46203	*Princess Margaret Rose*	Princess	4-6-2	Midland Railway Centre
46229	*Duchess of Hamilton*	Coronation	4-6-2	National Railway Museum
46233	*Duchess of Sutherland*	Coronation	4-6-2	Midland Railway Centre
46235	*City of Birmingham*	Coronation	4-6-2	Millenium Point, Birmingham
46428		2MT	2-6-0	East Lancs Railway
46441		2MT	2-6-0	Lakeside & Haverthwaite Railway
46443		2MT	2-6-0	Severn Valley Railway
46447		2MT	2-6-0	East Somerset Railway
46464		2MT	2-6-0	Bridge of Dun
46512		2MT	2-6-0	Strathspey Railway
46521		2MT	2-6-0	Great Central Railway
47279		Jinty	0-6-0T	Keighley & Worth Valley Railway
47298		Jinty	0-6-0T	Bury
47324		Jinty	0-6-0T	East Lancs Railway
47327		Jinty	0-6-0T	Midland Railway Centre
47357		Jinty	0-6-0T	Midland Railway Centre
47383		Jinty	0-6-0T	Severn Valley Railway
47406		Jinty	0-6-0T	Ecclesbourne Valley Railway
47445		Jinty	0-6-0T	Midland Railway Centre
47493		Jinty	0-6-0T	Spa Valley Railway
47564		Jinty	0-6-0T	Midland Railway Centre
48151		8F	2-8-0	Carnforth
48173		8F	2-8-0	Churnet Valley Railway
48274		8F	2-8-0	Great Central Railway-N (Ex-Turkey)
48305		8F	2-8-0	Great Central Railway
48431		8F	2-8-0	Keighley & Worth Valley Railway
48624		8F	2-8-0	Great Central Railway
48773		8F	2-8-0	Severn Valley Railway
49395		7F	0-8-0	National Railway Museum
50621		LYR	2-4-2T	National Railway Museum

51218		LYR	0-4-0ST	Keighley & Worth Valley Railway
52044		LYR	0-6-0	Keighley & Worth Valley Railway
52322		LYR	0-6-0	East Lancs Railway
53808 (88)		7F	2-8-0	West Somerset Railway
53809		7F	2-8-0	Midland Railway, Butterley
55189			0-4-4T	Scottish Railway Pres Society
57566			0-6-0	Strathspey Railway
58850			0-6-0T	Barrow Hill
58926			0-6-2T	Keighley & Worth Valley Railway
11243			0-4-0ST	Ribble Steam Railway
11456		752	0-6-0ST	Keighley & Worth Valley Railway
123			4-2-2	Riverside Museum, Glasgow
103			4-6-0	Riverside Museum, Glasgow
158A			2-4-0	Midland Railway Centre
419			0-4-4T	Bo'ness and Kinneil
673		Spinner	4-2-2	National Railway Museum
828		812	0-6-0	Strathspey Railway
2271 (NSR 2)			0-6-2T	National Railway Museum at Foxfield
1439			0-4-0ST	NRM at Ribble Steam Railway
49	*Columbine*		2-2-2	Science Museum
3	*Coppernob*	FR	0-4-0	National Railway Museum
FR20			0-4-0	Ribble Valley Steam Railway
FR25			0-4-0ST	Ribble Valley Railway
57	*Lion*	L&M	0-4-2	Liverpool Museum
5	*Cecil Raikes*		0-6-4T	Liverpool Museum

London North Eastern
and constitute companies

No.	Name	Class	Wheel Arrangement	Location
GNR 1		Stirling	4-2-2	National Railway Museum
66	*Aerolite*	X1	2-2-4T	National Railway Museum
251		C1	4-4-2	National Railway Museum
910	*Fletcher*		2-4-0	NRM at Kirkby Stephen East
990	*Henry Oakley*	C2	4-4-2	National Railway Museum
1275		1001	0-6-0	National Railway Museum
1310		Y7	0-4-0T	Middleton Railway
1463	*Tennant*	E5	2-4-0	NRM at Darlington
1621		D17	4-4-0	National Railway Museum
60007	*Sir Nigel Gresley*	A4	4-6-2	North Yorkshire Moors Railway
60008	*Dwight D Eisenhower*	A4	4-6-2	Green Bay, Wisconsin, USA
60009	*Union of South Africa*	A4	4-6-2	Severn Valley Railway
60010	*Dominion of Canada*	A4	4-6-2	Canadian Railway Museum
60019	*Bittern*	A4	4-6-2	Loco Storage, Margate
60022	*Mallard*	A4	4-6-2	National Railway Museum
60103	*Flying Scotsman*	A3	4-6-2	National Railway Museum
60532	*Blue Peter*	A2	4-6-2	LNWR Crewe
60800	*Green Arrow*	V2	2-6-2	National Railway Museum
61264		B1	4-6-0	North Yorkshire Moors Railway
61306	*Mayflower*	B1	4-6-0	WCRC Southall
61572		B12	4-6-0	North Norfolk Railway
61994	*Great Marquess*	K4	2-6-0	Severn Valley Railway
62005		K1	2-6-0	North Yorkshire Moors Railway
62277	*Gordon Highlander*	D40	4-4-0	Glasgow Transport Museum
62469	*Glen Douglas*	D34	4-4-0	Scottish Railway Pres Society
62660	*Butler Henderson*	D11	4-4-0	NRM at Great Central Railway
62712	*Morayshire*	D49	4-4-0	Scottish Railway Pres Society
62785		E4	2-4-0	Bressingham
63395		Q6	0-8-0	North Yorkshire Moors Railway
63460		Q7	0-8-0	NRM at Darlington Museum
63601		O4	2-8-0	Great Central Railway
65033		J21	0-6-0	Stainmore Railway
65243	*Maude*	J36	0-6-0	Scottish Railway Pres Society
65462		J15	0-6-0	North Norfolk Railway

65567	J17	0-6-0	NRM at Barrow Hill
65894	J27	0-6-0	North Yorkshire Moors Railway
68011	J94	0-6-0ST	In Belgium
68030	J94	0-6-0ST	Churnet Valley Railway
68077	J94	0-6-0ST	Spa Valley Railway
68088	Y7	0-4-0T	Great Central Railway
68095	Y9	0-4-0ST	Scottish Railway Pres Society
68153	Y1/2	4w	Middleton Railway
68633	J69	0-6-0T	National Railway Museum
68846	J52	0-6-0ST	NRM at Great Central Railway
69023	J72	0-6-0T	Wensleydale Railway
69523	N2	0-6-2T	North Norfolk Railway
69621	N7	0-6-2T	EAR

British Railways

No.	Name	Class	Wheel Arrangement	Location
70000	*Britannia*	Britannia	4-6-2	Crewe
70013	*Oliver Cromwell*	Britannia	4-6-2	Great Central Railway
71000	*Duke of Gloucester*		4-6-2	Tyseley Museum
73050	*City of Peterborough*	Class 5	4-6-0	Nene Valley Railway
73082	*Camelot*	Class 5	4-6-0	Bluebell Railway
73096	*Merlin*	Class 5	4-6-0	Mid-Hants Railway
73129		Class 5	4-6-0	Midland Railway Centre
73156		Class 5	4-6-0	Great Central Railway
75014		Class 4	4-6-0	Dartmouth Steam Railway
75027		Class 4	4-6-0	Bluebell Railway
75029	*The Green Knight*	Class 4	4-6-0	North Yorkshire Moors Railway
75069		Class 4	4-6-0	Severn Valley Railway
75078		Class 4	4-6-0	Keighley & Worth Valley Railway
75079		Class 4	4-6-0	Mid-Hants Railway
76017		Class 4	2-6-0	Mid-Hants Railway
76077		Class 4	2-6-0	Gloucestershire Warwickshire Railway
76079		Class 4	2-6-0	North Yorkshire Moors Railway
76084		Class 4	2-6-0	North Norfolk Railway
78018		Class 2	2-6-0	Great Central Railway
78019		Class 2	2-6-0	Great Central Railway
78022		Class 2	2-6-0	Keighley & Worth Valley Railway
80002		Class 4	2-6-4T	Keighley & Worth Valley Railway
80064		Class 4	2-6-4T	Bluebell Railway
80072		Class 4	2-6-4T	Llangollen Railway
80078		Class 4	2-6-4T	Mangapps Farm
80079		Class 4	2-6-4T	Severn Valley Railway
80080		Class 4	2-6-4T	Midland Railway Centre
80097		Class 4	2-6-4T	East Lancs Railway
80098		Class 4	2-6-4T	Midland Railway Centre
80100		Class 4	2-6-4T	Bluebell Railway
80104		Class 4	2-6-4T	Swanage Railway
80105		Class 4	2-6-4T	Scottish Railway Pres Society
80135		Class 4	2-6-4T	North Yorkshire Moors Railway
80136		Class 4	2-6-4T	North Yorkshire Moors Railway
80150		Class 4	2-6-4T	Mid-Hants Railway
80151		Class 4	2-6-4T	Bluebell Railway
90733		WD	2-10-0	Keighley & Worth Valley Railway
90775		WD	2-10-0	North Norfolk Railway (Ex Greece)
600	*Gordon*	WD	2-10-0	Severn Valley Railway
92134		9F	2-10-0	North Yorkshire Moors Railway
92203	*Black Prince*	9F	2-10-0	North Norfolk Railway
92207		9F	2-10-0	Shillingstone Station
92212		9F	2-10-0	Mid-Hants Railway
92214	*Lieicester City*	9F	2-10-0	Great Central Railway
92219		9F	2-10-0	Wensleydale Railway
92220	*Evening Star*	9F	2-10-0	National Railway Museum
92240		9F	2-10-0	Bluebell Railway
92245		9F	2-10-0	Barry Island Railway

Several preserved steam locomotives have been allocated five-digit TOPS numbers to allow their operation over the National Network. The numbers allocated are shown below; not all locos may currently be authorised for use over Network Rail metals.

TOPS No.	Railway No.	Type	Name
98150	1450	GWR 14xx	
98166	1466	GWR 14xx	
98186	686	0-6-0T	*Lady Armaghdale*
98212	41312	LMS 2MT	
98219	55189	CR 0-4-4T	
98221	46521	LMS 2MT	
98238	1638	GWR 16xx	
98240	3440	GWR 34xx	*City of Truro*
98241	46441	LMS 2MT	
98243	46443	LMS 2MT	
98253	30053	SR M7	
98254	58926	LNWR 2F	
98273	65243	NBR J36	*Maude*
98315	7715	GWR 57xx	
98321	69621	GER N7	*A. J. Hill*
98372	30072	SR USA	
98400	41000	LMS 4P	
98406	43106	LMS 4MT	
98414	75014	BR 4MT	
98425	7325	GWR 7321	
98426	31625	SR U	
98427	44027	LMS 4F	
98435	80135	BR 4MT	
98455	4555	GWR 45xx	
98457	9600	GWR 8750	
98460	7760	GWR 57xx	
98466	9466	GWR 94xx	
98469	75069	BR 4MT	
98472	5572	GWR 4575	
98476	76079	BR 4MT	
98478	68078	WD 4F	
98479	80079	BR 4MT	
98480	80080	BR 4MT	
98482	3882	0-6-0ST	*Barbara*
98484	76084	BR 4MT	
98488	4588	GWR 4575	
98494	65894	LNER J27	
98498	80098	BR 4MT	
98500	45000	LMS 5MT	
98502	7802	GWR 78xx	*Bradley Manor*
98505	45305	LMS 5MT	*Alderman A E Draper*
98507	45407	LMS 5MT	*Lancashire Fusilier*
98510	45110	LMS 5MT	
98512	7812	GWR 78xx	*Erlestoke Manor*
98519	7819	GWR 78xx	*Hinton Manor*
98525	45025	LMS 5MT	
98526	30925	SR V	*Cheltenham*
98529	73129	BR 5MT	
98530	4930	GWR 49xx	*Hagley Hall*
98531	45231	LMS 5MT	*Sherwood Forester*
98532	44932	LMS 5MT	
98536	4936	GWR 49xx	*Kinlet Hall*
98549	4965	GWR 49xx	*Rood Ashton Hall*
98553	4953	GWR 49xx	*Pitchford Hall*
98560	6960	GWR 6959	*Raveningham Hall*
98564	61264	LNER B1	
98565	42765	LMS 5MT	
98567	44767	LMS 5MT	*George Stephenson*
98568	42968	LMS 5MT	
98571	44871	LMS 5MT	
98572	5972	GWR 49xx	*Olton Hall*
98577	30777	SR N15	*Sir Lamiel*
98596	73096	BR 5MT	
98598	6998	GWR 6959	*Burton Agnes Hall*
98605	62005	LNER K1	
98628	30828	SR S15	
98641	30841	SR S15	
98642	61994	LNER K4	*The Great Marquess*
98690	45690	LMS 6P5F	*Leander*
98693	45593	LMS 6P5F	*Kolhapur*
98696	45596	LMS 6P5F	*Bahamas*
98699	45699	LMS 6P5F	*Galatea*
98700	70000	BR 7P	*Britannia*
98701	34101	SR WC	*Hartland*
98709	53809	SDJR 7F	
98713	70013	BR 7P	*Oliver Cromwell*
98715	46115	LMS 7P	*Scots Guardsman*
98716	34016	SR WC	*Bodmin*
98727	34027	SR WC	*Taw Valley*
98728	5029	GWR 4073	*Nunney Castle*
98729	7029	BR 4073	*Clun Castle*
98746	34046	SR WC	*Braunton*
98750	30850	SR LN	*Lord Nelson*
98751	5051	GWR 4073	*Earl Bathurst*
98767	34067	SR BB	*Tangmere*
98771	60800	LNER V2	*Green Arrow*
98772	34072	SR BB	*257 Squadron*
98780	5080	GWR 4073	*Defiant*
98792	34092	SR WC	*City of Wells*
98800	6000	GWR 60xx	*King George V*
98801	46201	LMS 8P	*Princess Elizabeth*
98802	71000	BR 8P	*Duke of Gloucester*
98803	46203	LMS 8P	*Princess Margaret Rose*
98805	35005	SR MN	*Canadian Pacific*
98809	60009	LNER A4	*Union of South Africa*
98824	6024	GWR 60xx	*King Edward I*
98828	35028	BR MN	*Clan Line*
98829	46229	LMS 8P	*Duchess of Hamilton*
98832	60532	LNER A2	*Blue Peter*
98834	46233	LMS 8P	*Duchess of Sutherland*
98851	48151	LMS 8F	
98857	2857	GWR 28xx	
98863	60163	LNER A1	*Tornado*
98868	60022	LNER A4	*Mallard*
98872	60103	LNER A3	*Flying Scotsman*
98873	48773	LMS 8F	
98898	60007	LNER A4	*Sir Nigel Gresley*
98920	92220	BR 9F	*Evening Star*

Class 89 No.	BR TOPS No.	Type	Name
89100	20050	Class 20	-
89101	20001	Class 20	-
89127	20227	Class 20	-
89188	20188	Class 20	-
89200	31018	Class 31	-
89204	26004	Class 26	-
89210	27059	Class 27	-
89212	LT 12	LTa	*Sarah Siddons*
89218	D5910	Class 23	-
89223	25173	Class 25	-
89233	25283	Class 25	-
89247	27001	Class 27	-
89254	24054	Class 24	-
89259	25309	Class 25	-
89261	24061	Class 24	-
89262	25262	Class 25	-
89280	31162	Class 31	-
89317	D7017	Class 35	-
89376	D7076	Class 35	-
89400	E27000	Class 77	*Electra*
89401	47401	Class 47	*North Eastern*
89402	50002	Class 50	*Superb*
89403	71001	Class 71	-
89404	44004	Class 44	*Great Gable*
89405	47117	Class 47	-
89412	40012	Class 40	*Aureol*
89413	D1013	Class 52	*Western Ranger*
89415	50015	Class 50	*Valiant*
89416	D1015	Class 52	*Western Champion*
89417	50017	Class 50	*Royal Oak*
89420	45108	Class 45	-
89421	D821	Class 42	*Greyhound*
89422	50021	Class 50	*Rodney*
89423	45125	Class 45	-
89424	D1023	Class 52	*Western Fusilier*
89427	50027	Class 50	*Lion*
89431	50031	Class 50	*Hood*
89432	D832	Class 42	*Onslaught*
89435	40135	Class 40	-
89440	45133	Class 45	-
89441	D1041	Class 52	*Western Prince*
89442	47192	Class 47	-
89443	50042	Class 50	*Triumph*
89444	50044	Class 50	*Exeter*
89445	40145	Class 40	-
89448	D1048	Class 52	*Western Lady*
89449	50049	Class 50	*Defiance*
89453	45041	Class 45	*Royal Tank Regiment*
89460	45060	Class 45	*Sherwood Forester*
89462	D1062	Class 52	*Western Courier*
89466	47449	Class 47	-
89472	46035	Class 46	*Ixion*
89500	55022	Class 55	*Royal Scots Grey*
89502	55002	Class 55	*The King's Own Yorkshire Light Infantry*
89503	81002	Class 81	-
89509	55009	Class 55	*Alycidon*
89515	55015	Class 55	*Tulyar*
89516	55016	Class 55	*Gordon Highlander*
89519	55019	Class 55	*Royal Highland Fusilier*
89523	DP1	Proto	*Deltic*
89535	83012	Class 83	-
89561	85101	Class 85	-

Below: *The preserved 'Hastings' DEMU set, based at St Leonards near Hastings and owned by Hastings Diesels Ltd is frequently used on main line charters. The owners have enough vehicles to form two six-vehicle Hastings sets when all are restored. At present the set usually operates with a CEP vehicle and a BIG buffet car from EMU sets. Led by vehicle S60116, No. 1001 is seen at Paignton in summer 2018 with the South Devon Coaster charter.* **Antony Christie**

Above: *Merchant Navy Locomotive Preservation Society owned No. 35028 Clan Line is usually based at Stewarts Lane and operates the steam powered legs of the Belmond/VSOE Pullman. Working in tandem with DB Pullman-liveried Class 67 No. 67024, Clan Line pulls into London Victoria with the luxury train.* **Antony Christie**

Below: *Very popular for main line charter use are the preserved Class 50s, Nos. 50007 and 50049 which currently hold main line certification. The pair look especially pleasing to photograph when powering the restored blue and grey-liveried Mk2 passenger set, as shown here of the pair leading 'The Cumbrian Hoovers' through Warrington Bank Quay.* **Antony Christie**

Above: *Built in the mid 1890s, Webb Coat Tank 0-6-2T No. 1054 is superbly restored by the Keighley & Worth Valley Railway, and currently carries all black livery with its LNWR number. Over its years in preservation the loco has carried its BR identity 58926 and its LMS No. 7799.* **Antony Christie**

Below: *One of the most unusual steam powered vehicles to operate over Network Rail tracks in recent years is the superbly restored Great Western steam Rail Motor No. 93, stored at Didcot. The amazing vehicle is seen from its non-steam end on the Liskeard to Looe branch in Cornwall at Terras Crossing.* **Antony Christie**

Above: *A preservation masterpiece is South Eastern & Chatham Railway Class 01 No. 65, built in 1896 at Ashford Works for South Eastern freight operations. It later carried the numbers 1065 and BR No. 31065 and was withdrawn from service in the early 1960s and entered preservation. For many years the loco has been housed at the Bluebell Railway in Sussex. This view shows the loco with a SECR demonstration freight at Horstead Keynes.* **Antony Christie**

Below: *Another former South Eastern and Chatham loco is P class 0-6-0T No. 323, built at Ashford Works in July 1910 and was one of a small batch being the South Eastern's answer to the LBSCR A1x class. No. 31323 as it became under BR remained in traffic mainly in the Dover area until July 1960 when it was withdrawn and preserved. The loco is currently based on the Bluebell Railway, where it has been repainted in blue livery and named* Bluebell. *It is seen on loan to the Spa Valley Line.* **Antony Christie**

Above: *LMS design Ivatt Class 2 2-6-0 No. 46521 was in fact built by BR at Swindon works in March 1953, it remained in traffic until October 1966. It is now preserved on the Great Central Railway and is seen at Quorn and Woodhouse in September 2018.* **Antony Christie**

Below: *1957-built BR Standard 4MT 2-6-0 No. 76079, built in February 1957 at BR Horwich Works and withdrawn just 10 years later, is now preserved at the North Yorkshire Moors Railway. The loco is seen at Grosmont.* **Antony Christie**

Preserved site codes

ACL	AC Locomotive Group
ALY	Allelys, Studley
APF	Appleby-Frodingham RPS
AVR	Avon Valley Railway
BAT	Battlefield Line
BEL	5BEL Trust Barrow Hill
BHR	Barrow Hill Roundhouse
BIR	Barry Island Railway
BKR	Bo'ness & Kinneil Railway
BLU	Bluebell Railway
BRC	Buckinghamshire Railway Centre
BRM	Birmingham Railway Museum, Tyseley
BVR	Bridgend Valleys Railway
BWR	Bodmin & Wenford Railway
CAN	Canton (Pullman Rail)
CHS	Chasewater Railway
COL	Colne Valley Railway
C4P	Class 40 Preservation Society
CPR	Chinnor & Princes Risborough Railway
CRB	Caledonian Railway, Brechin
CRT	Cambrian Railway Trust
CVR	Churnet Valley Railway
CWR	Cholsey & Wallingford Railway
DAR	Dartmoor Railway
DEE	Royal Deeside Railway
DER	Derwent Valley Railway
DFR	Dean Forest Railway
DID	Didcot Railway Centre
EAR	East Anglian Railway Museum
ECC	Ecclesbourne Valley Railway
EDR	Eden Valley Railway
EHC	Elsecar Heritage Centre
EHD	Eastleigh DBS Depot
EKR	East Kent Railway
ELR	East Lancashire Railway
EMB	Embsay Steam Railway
EPO	Epping and Ongar Railway
FHL	Fawley Hall (private)
FIN	Finmere Station, Oxfordshire
GCN	Great Central Railway (North)
GCR	Great Central Railway
GKR	Graham Kirk Rail
GWI	Gwili Railway
GWR	Gloucestershire Warwickshire Railway
HAD	Hastings Diesels
IOW	Isle of Wight Railway
IVT	Ivatt Diesel Preservation
KEI	Keith & Dufftown Railway
KES	Kent & East Sussex Railway
KIN	MoD Kineton
KWV	Keighley & Worth Valley Railway
LAN	Llangollen Railway
LDL	Lavender Line
LHG	LH Group Services, Burton
LHR	Lakeside & Haverthwaite Railway
LNW	London & North Western, Crewe
LWR	Lincolnshire Wolds Railway
MET	Methill (Private)
MFM	Mangapps Farm Railway Museum
MHR	Mid Hants Railway
MID	Middleton Railway
MLM	Motorail, Long Marston
MNF	Mid-Norfolk Railway
MOR	Moreton-on-Lugg
MRC	Middleton Railway Centre
MSM	Museum of Science & Industry, Manchester
MSR	Midsomer Norton
NHD	Newton Heath Depot
NIR	Northamptonshire Ironstone Railway
NLR	Northampton & Lamport Railway
NNR	North Norfolk Railway
NRM	National Railway Museum, York
NRS	National Railway Museum, Shildon
NYM	North Yorkshire Moors Railway
PBR	Pontypool & Blaenavon Railway
PDR	Paignton & Dartmouth Railway
PRL	Peak Rail
PVR	Plym Valley Railway
RAC	Railway Age, Crewe
RAM	Rampart, Derby
RHW	Rushden, Higham & Wellingborough Railway
RIB	Ribble Steam Railway
RIP	Rippingdale Station
ROW	Rowley Mill
RST	Rushden Station Transport Museum
SEL	St Leonards Railway Engineering
SLN	Stewarts Lane Depot
SPV	Spa Valley Railway
SRC	Stainmore Railway Co
STR	Strathspey Railway
SVR	Severn Valley Railway
SWI	Swindon & Cricklade Railway
SWN	Swanage Railway
TEB	Friends of 502 Group, Tebay
TEL	Telford Horsehay Steam Trust
THK	Throckmorton Airfield
TLW	Tyseley Locomotive Works
TIT	Titley Junction
TSR	Telford Steam Railway
TYN	North Tyneside Railway
VBR	Vale of Berkeley Railway
VOG	Vale of Glamorgan Railway
WAS	Washwood Heath
WCR	West Coast Railway Co
WED	Weardale Railway
WEN	Wensleydale Railway
WPH	Walthamstow Pump House
WST	West Somerset Railway
XXX	Private unspecified site
YEO	Yeovil Railway Centre

Status

OPR	Operational
OPR	Operational main-line certified
RES	Under restoration
STC	Static exhibit
STO	Stored

Also by Colin J Marsden

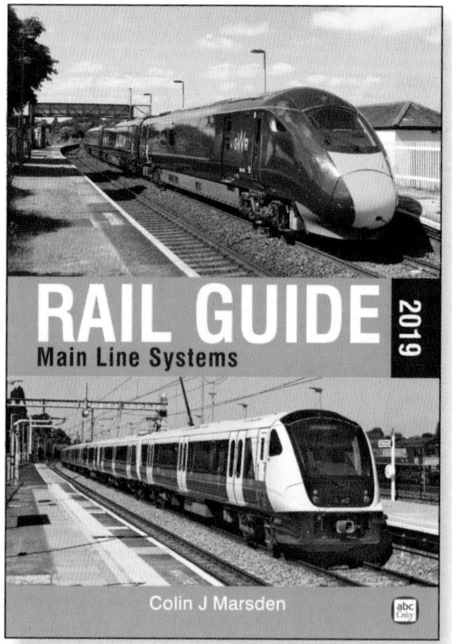

abc Rail Guide 2019

Main Line Systems

abc Rail Guide has established itself as the most comprehensive, detailed, accurate and reliable guide to the railway networks of the British Isles. The 2019 edition of this best-selling annual publication has been thoroughly revised and updated and provides listings in operator order of the locomotives, multiple units and stock used on the railways of Britain and Ireland.

Entries are separately cross-referenced to their operators delivering the best single volume reference source on the contemporary railway scene. Portable, up to date, concise, easy to use, with Train Operating Company route maps and colour photographs throughout, this is the essential guide for all railway enthusiasts seeking to keep up to speed with the dynamic and rapidly changing railway landscape.

Hardback
210mm x 148mm
328 pages
ISBN: 9781910809556
£22.50

Available from all good bookshops

Crécy Publishing Ltd
www.crecy.co.uk